Giving Our Hearts Away: Native American Survival

A Mission Study for 2008-2009
by Thom White Wolf Fassett

with Study Guide
by Brenda Connelly

Women's Division • General Board of Global Ministries • The United Methodist Church

Photo Credits:
Thom White Wolf Fassett: pp. 6, 7, 8, 35
Alvin Deer: p. 48
Carol Lakota Eastin: p. 54

Giving Our Hearts Away: Native American Survival

A publication of the Women's Division, General Board of Global Ministries, The United Methodist Church

ISBN# 978-1-933663-30-2

Library of Congress Control Number 2007943648

TABLE OF CONTENTS

INTRODUCTION

The title of this book was inspired by a communication written by Ferdinand Columbus to his sovereigns on one of his four voyages to the "new world." He wrote that the Natives "... were a kind, gentle and generous people who would give him their hearts if he asked them to do so."[1] At first it wasn't their hearts for which he asked, but their gold. But before Columbus concluded his excursions into the Americas, he set into motion such depravations as would astound modern readers of history by demanding not only gold, but also the hearts and lives of the indigenous peoples. This process continues even in our own times as military forces, sophisticated weaponry and legal actions take the very hearts of Native peoples by claiming their land–the center of Native spiritual reality.

I write unambiguously as a Christian and as a Native American. The apparent contradictions between these two identities will be obvious as we explore history and examine contemporary conditions that would seem to pit each against the other. The dispossession of Native Americans by an immigrant population claiming to be God's chosen people who had the right to inherit a virgin land is the central contradictory theme that will be repeated throughout our study. The church's role in the subjugation of America's Native people is palpable. Only as we immerse ourselves in the history of the United States and the role of the Christian church in the societies of Native Americans will we be able to emerge with a new understanding of our own identity as people of faith. Then we have the possibility of gaining a healthy perspective on our responsibility in the challenges to Native American survival. We are, as writer Alice Walker phrased it, "looking backward toward the future."

As I sat writing this introduction in my farmhouse overlooking Seneca Lake in Western New York State, I gazed at the land below me, the ancestral land of my ancient family, the Senecas.[2] To the east stretches the traditional homeland of the Cayugas–another nation of the Six Nations Iroquois. This territory has been under legal contention for nearly two hundred years as the Cayugas have attempted to reclaim their land through U.S. courts. Over a period of time, a vigilante group formed to defend the current owners of the land from the loss of their property. Realtors instilled fear in the residents with claims of lower property values and the threat of the loss of their livelihoods. This ongoing struggle is a vestige of the Non-Intercourse Act of 1807. A recent 2006 Supreme Court decision denied the Cayuga claim and set aside, if not terminated, the just expectations of a Native nation depending on the United States to honor a solemn ancient agreement. This is but one example of the current challenges facing both the Native and non-Native worlds in the United States, demonstrating that ancient history is as relevant and up-to-date to Native tribes and nations as a freshly peeled orange.

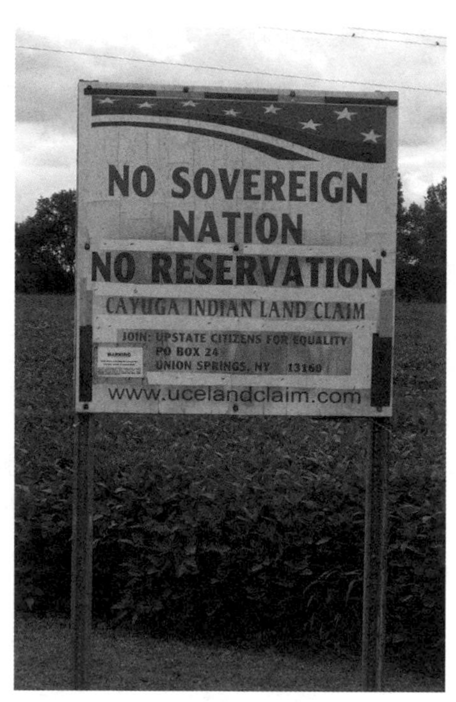

In 1779 in my own homeland during the Revolutionary War, General John Sullivan moved through this territory with his troops, burning longhouses and destroying cornfields and orchards as a means of vanquishing the Six Nations, including the Senecas and Cayugas. His objective was to clear the Northwest Territories–as they were then known–of savages and hostile tribal peoples to provide unspoiled tracts of land to new immigrants. Already forgotten was the 1787 Northwest Ordinance that provided that

> " …the utmost good faith shall always be observed toward the Indians. Their land and properties shall never be taken from them without their consent. In their property rights and liberty, they shall never be invaded or disturbed, unless in just

and lawful wars authorized by Congress. The laws founded in justice and humanity shall from time to time be made for preventing wrongs done to them and for preserving peace and friendship with them..."[3]

Sullivan's campaign was successful. Vast territories were handed over to a land-hungry immigrant population who cleared the forests, burned stumps and subsequently built houses, plowed fields for crops and raised herds of cattle. Many of General Sullivan's troops returned to this territory to claim their military prize of land as a reward for fighting in the American Revolution. As we shall see, Native Americans were always hindrances to these new "nation builders" as they attempted to "civilize" them and extinguish their claims to their homelands. Generally, there is little patience for dealing with aboriginal land claims because of the wide perception that "Indians" don't exist today and that the events of the past are ancient history.

Among the very first immigrant settlers to this newly nationalized land came the family who would–some one hundred and fifty years later–adopt me as their own. Even as I looked from my farmhouse, I could see the little one-room round schoolhouse they and others used to educate their children. One of my grandfathers, from whom I received my Christian name, escaped through a window of that schoolhouse as a little boy, never to return. As an adult he worked for the railroad that carried to market the fruits and harvests of the sons and daughters of the original immigrant population. I tell this story because it captures a snapshot of history that illustrates the contemporary realities facing American Indian people of my generation and the generations of assimilated, urbanized sisters and brothers coming after me. This is an oft-repeated story of the relationship between Indians and the new European settlers. The impact this historical experience is still felt by contemporary generations of families and communities.

What became of the sons and daughters of the first peoples or, as early historians called them, the "Noble Savages?" The Declaration of Independence, so recently celebrated in 1776, gave George Washington (and under his orders, General Sullivan) license to hunt and remove the first peoples from their homes, depriving them of their independence. In later documents that would define the new republic of The United States of America, African Americans would be counted as 3/5ths human beings, while Native Americans were declared savages. This term for Native Americans would hold official currency through the presidency of Theodore Roosevelt.

The past must be used as a backdrop, not an indictment.

How does Christian America rationalize the treatment of a people who were decimated by new immigrant cultures and religious values, whose lands were seen as a commodity of commerce and not as a sacred living organism? Many church members will decry the implications of these questions and perhaps assign them to some pagan notion belonging to a theology born of heathen ignorance. The true story, never found in textbooks of American history, tests our credibility while challenging our very "ground of being" as disciples of Jesus Christ. This is the nature of our current study.

It is the fortune of this generation to be able to listen attentively to Native Americans and to begin to understand what they are saying, to comprehend their points of view as a unique component of our American population. The past must be used as a backdrop, not an indictment. But the backdrop explains most of what we must know about the present-day condition of Native peoples. We are exploring ways of seeing and hearing and praying in a context that may surprise some students of this text. Native

American theology will certainly alarm some modern Christians as we explore the cultural practices of honoring Mother Earth and praying for all of creation–including the four leggeds, the two leggeds, the winged ones and the water creatures. These practices have often been declared pantheistic by Western civilization. Note the opening traditional prayer found in the "First Words" section at the beginning of this study and compare it with the first few lines from the first chapter of John. "The earth is the Lord's and all that is in it, the world, and those who live in it," (Psalm24:1a), translated into Native American spiritual practice, appropriately captures the spirit of a people and of the hundreds of Native nations that once inhabited what is now the United States—people who continue to honor the original instructions of the Creator. The sacredness of creation is a theme that will guide us as we come to understand Native spirituality and perhaps our own.

The sacredness of creation is a theme that will guide us as we come to understand Native spirituality and perhaps our own.

The role of the church and the state in the elimination of Native Americans as a unique people is captured in the troubling recitation of methods employed to force Native people to cease being who they are and to conform to the dominant society. At the same time Native people were promised that the government would support their right to survive as Native people and to live within their own culture. Native people have survived to this day at great cost. The struggle has produced decades of confusion, hopelessness and poverty, and social and geographical displacement. But it has also generated a continuing determination to take control of their own lives and, like all free Americans, to manage and control their own destiny. The question for this generation is whether this nation, 516 years after the landing of the Pinta, Nina and the Santa Maria, is now mature enough and secure enough to tolerate—even encourage within the larger culture—societies of Native peoples who wish to maintain their own unique tribal governments, cultures and spiritual values. The question before the church today is whether it is strong enough to bring about a change in the United States and around the world where indigenous peoples have been decimated and left victims of dominant Western economies or of the imposition of oppressive cultural values.

Indian law scholar Felix Cohen once said: "If we fight for civil liberties for our side, we show that we believe not in civil liberties but in our side. But when those of us who never were Indians and never expect to be Indians fight for the Indian cause of self-government, we are fighting for something that is not limited by accidents of race and creed and birth; we are fighting for what Las Casas, Vitoria and Pope Paul III called the integrity of salvation of our own souls. We are fighting for what Jefferson called the basic rights of man. We are fighting for the last best hope of earth. And these are causes which should carry us through many defeats."[4]

The question before the church today is whether it is strong enough to bring about a change in the United States and around the world where indigenous peoples have been decimated and left victims of dominant Western economies or of the imposition of oppressive cultural values.

The "winning of Independence" in 1783 transferred power and authority to basically White Americans who were now organized as a new nation while foreclosing on the independence of Native nations. Themes of Manifest Destiny have been at play since the earliest explorations of the Americas. Columbus did not spawn this long history of oppression against America's indigenous people. He was only one foot soldier in the invading armies of conquering immigrants thirsting for wealth and freedom, who worshiped God, carrying the cross and gun, and were intent on "discovering" and subduing the so-called wilderness of the Americas. The cross and the gun led to European domination and to the corruption of Native cultures. Perhaps by that time Christianity had lost its way as it became essentially a state religion. This created a spiritual vacuum in the West that eventually manifested itself in exploration, conquest, conversion and greed.

As scholars have noted before, this was an era when Christians had forgotten the wilderness days of the Israelites and the spiritual impulses that married them to the land. They had forgotten the warnings of Yahweh not to move the borders of land established by former generations (Deuteronomy 19:14). Among "savages", the new Christian immigrants witnessed a spiritual phenomenon they had long since forgotten, one that emanated from their own Biblical traditions and the creation themes in their own holy texts. Ironically, royal decrees from abroad and treaties and diplomatic negotiations with tribal nations would acknowledge the sacred nature of agreements and would concede, at least for a short time, the "nationhood" of the Native entities. In his book *Studies in Classic American Literature*, D. H. Lawrence would observe that the curious thing about the Spirit of Place is the fact that no place exerts its full influence upon the newcomer until the old inhabitant is dead or absorbed.

The Christian Messiah was betrayed not by the message preached by his Western missionaries but by the manner in which they sought to convert the "heathen." The civilization created by the missionaries of the cross seemed to substitute dogma for true belief. The emphasis was less on behavior as witnessed by the acts of the Christian settlers than it was on committing to the rubrics of the *Book of Common Prayer* or the theocratic rules and laws of the recently established colonies. Many missiologists of our time agree that it was the imposition of Western Christianity on indigenous cultures that robbed them of their spiritual lives. Where Christianity was allowed to become "indigenized," as is now occurring in Africa, the phenomenon flourished and became integral to Native spirituality. This process of indigenization, now emerging in Native churches in the United States, may consist simply of the use of drums or the symbolic colors of the four directions of the universe or a particular dance in the context of Christian worship. However, the truest adaptation of Christianity into the Indian context is in the Native American Church. This is an organized movement that employs the use of peyote as the sacramental medium.

Perhaps our generation will free captive Native nations as we learn from Native peoples and discover spiritual values that will see us through our own current spiritual emergency, save our embattled earth and enable humankind to live as one with creation and all living creatures within it–including ourselves.

The use such terms as "Indian," "Native," "Native American," "Amerind," and others always imposes a challenge for us because there are inconsistent usages among Native people. However, for this study, the terms "Indian", "Native", "American Indian" and "Native American" will be used interchangeably. Two exceptions exist in the cases of Native Alaskans and Native Hawaiians. I prefer the term "Native" but am strongly drawn to use "Indian." Although historically faulty, I can still hear my traditional Lakota father, Spotted Horse, declaring that we are "Indian" because that is the language used in the treaties and other legal agreements between the United States and tribal nations, bands and aboriginal organizations.

Unless one knows the precise name used by tribal people for themselves, almost anything expressed in the Spanish, English or French languages will be incorrect and merely repeat the names given those Native nations by immigrant invaders. For example, most of us are aware of the northern plains people called the "Sioux." However, that is a French term. The people call themselves either Lakota, Nakota or Dakota, depending on which social grouping they are referencing. I am a Seneca belonging to a confederation of five other nations known as the Six Nations to the English, or as Iroquois to the French. We call ourselves the Haudenosaunee (the people of the Longhouse). Sometimes, some of us call ourselves the "Onkehonweh," the "real people." Our confederation is technically made up of the Seneca, Tuscarora, Onondaga, Cayuga, Oneida and Mohawk Nations. The Ho-Chunk Nation has been referred to as Winnebago.

The Navajo call themselves the Dene (or Dine') Who would know that the Creeks are Muskokee, or that Eskimos are Inuit or that Papagos are Tohono O'Odham? The examples continue through all of the nations. Suffice it to say, we will use Indian, Native American, American Indian and Native in our discussions.

As people of faith, we are careful to begin our meetings with a prayer or meditative reflections. As we commence our study, why should we do less as we prepare ourselves to consider religious perspectives, understandings of the movement of the Creator on people, history and time and our role in the realm of God? Recognizing the role of the creator in the lives and health of the people, the traditional opening prayer on pages 14-15 is recited by spiritual leaders of Six Nations (also known as Iroquois) at the beginning of each day and at the beginning of all meetings of the people. Listen to the words, listen to the sounds, listen to the heart of the cadence and imagine it to be the center of spiritual focus for this study.

God is the source of every element of life and supplies all of the helpers that sustain and nourish all of us. I call this scriptural declaration "God's giveaway." This phrase gives credence to the concept of "giveaway" or "Potlatch," practiced by most Indian nations and Native cultures. There is generally a widespread understanding among Native people that we own nothing. This applies to the land and all that God has made. Therefore, we give away those things that are needed by others as God or the Great Spirit gives to us all that we need. We share with others the creator's bountiful gifts to us. Even when we have little, we share what we have with others who have needs.

As immigrants arrived from afar in the early settlement days, they asked for a place to "spread their blankets" (as Seneca chief Red Jacket would one day recall). But these immigrants believed they owned the land being shared with them by the Indian population. In truth, Indians did not believe that they owned the land. It belonged to God, the Great Mystery, and they had no right to own the breast of Mother Earth. And so they shared it with others. In later days, when Indians claimed the land that had been taken from them—leaving them nothing for their own use—they were called "Indian givers." In 1976, an anti-Indian

"In the beginning was the Word, and the Word was with God, and the Word was God. He was in the beginning with God. All things came into being through him, and without him not one thing came into being. What has come into being in him was life, and the life was the light of all people. The light shines in the darkness, and the darkness did not overcome it."
John 1:1-5

Traditional Iroquois Prayer

We are gathered in this meeting place to tell what the Creator has done.

As it is our custom when we are gathered, we are to indicate a high regard for one another. We see that all of the people are healthy and happy and there have been few or no disasters, no or at least little illness. As we look about us we see that the first thing people do when they come together is that they greet one another before going about their business and so we put our minds together as one mind and greet one another.

We look about us and see the one we call our mother the earth. Mother earth is the one who is carrying on in the most ancient of ways, still following the original instructions of the Creator. She is the supporter of all feet and all of life and we see that all of these good things are coming to us from the earth and so let us put our minds together as one mind and extend a greeting and thanksgiving to our mother the earth.

Looking about us we see that there are many kinds of water beings on the earth. Some of them are flowing from the mountains and they speak to us with their many voices. We see also the rivers. They are sometimes deep and slow moving. Others are rushing with torrents of power. We also see the lakes and the great salt waters. As we look about we know they are strong and they lift our spirits when we see them. It is the waters we first use in the morning. They keep us clean and healthy. We also use these waters to cook. We know that all of these lives exist in the world because of the waters. Let us put our minds together as one mind and extend a greeting and thanksgiving.

As we continue looking about the earth, we see that there many things growing on the earth. There are plants and grasses that form a blanket or a carpet for our mother the earth. We know that we have been using these things to sustain our lives. We have used these things for medicines and they have helped us at all times. As we look about we realize these plants that grow from the earth help us to pick up our spirits with fine aroma and things of good nature that make us feel proud.

We see also the berries and we see all kinds of things we use as foods. We are always using these and without them, we would not be able to carry on in this world. There is a special berry that is the leader of the berry kingdom. We call it the strawberry. It is the first of the plant kingdom to bear its fruit after the long and cold winter. And we use it in our ceremonies and also as a medicine. And so we put our minds together as one mind and extend a greeting and thanksgiving to these plants that grow from the earth for our health.

There are the ones among us from the plant kingdom who are related to the women and we call them the three sisters–the corn, bean and squash. The corn, bean and squash should be included in ceremonies whenever the great thanksgiving is recited. They are the sustainers of our lives. They are the ones to whom we turn at all times during the year. And so to the three sisters, the corn, bean and squash, we put our minds together as one mind and extend a greeting and a thanksgiving.

As we look about, we see that there is all of the tree life living abundantly on this land. It is the trees that we use for our houses. Some of the trees provide us with fruits and others provide flowers that will brighten our spirits. There is a special tree on the earth, one that we might look at as the head tree or the leading tree; this is the maple tree. The first to awaken from the sleep of the winter and its sweet sap will be used in ceremonies. As to all the tree life growing on the land we put our minds together as one mind and extend a greeting and thanksgiving.

We see that there are the four legged ones wandering about on the earth, our cousins, the animals, as we are told, were put here as company for us two legged ones. They will provide us with food to eat and, sometimes, they will provide clothing for us to wear. They will provide us with knowledge about how we should go about on this earth. And so to the four legged animals, we put our minds together as one mind and extend a greeting and thanksgiving.

Looking towards the sky, we see that there are those with feathers, those of the bird kingdom. We know that there are many kinds that return to us to tell us of the warm winds blowing and with their songs they enlighten our spirits in the spring. They bring us a good thought and sometimes they bring us good messages and we look to them and we are given good feelings as we look at them. As we look high into the sky we see one that stands out above all others. It is the eagle. It is the eagle that flies the highest, it is the eagle that flies closest to the sun, the one whose feathers we use as one who comes closest to the Creator among those moving about on the earth. And so we know that it is the birds that are helping us moving about on the earth. And so to the birds, we put our minds together as one mind and extend a greeting and thanksgiving.

Again, as we look about us we see those who are always about us and always watching us—the ones we call our grandfathers, the four winds. It is the four winds that bring us the rains and will keep the air clean for us. We know it is the four directions they come from each with a certain time to be with us each year. They have carried on in the most ancient ways as the Creator has told them, carrying with them the clouds and the thunders that will give us water to drink. And we know that without our grandfathers, we would not be able to carry on in this world. And so let us put our minds together as one mind and extend a greeting and thanksgiving to our grandfathers the four winds.

We see that one we call our elder brother the sun, the daytime light. We know that it is our elder brother sun that is still carrying on the most ancient ways. He is still bringing warmth and light upon the land so that as we go about on the earth we will not bump into one another and cause conflicts and troubles. So let us put our minds together as one mind and extend a greeting and thanksgiving to our elder brother the sun.

As we look into the sky, we see there is another, the one we call the night time light, our grandmother, the moon. The moon will always follow the path across the sky as she fulfills the original instructions. It is she who is looking over all water life and every day, the waters will rise and fall according to the ancient ways. Whenever the plants grow they are growing by her power. We also know that it is grandmother moon who is the leader of all female life. She is the one who determines birth and every month she will renew her cycles, the cycles of the female life in this world, and so we want to put our minds together as one mind and extend a greeting and thanksgiving to our grandmother the moon.

As we look even higher into the sky we see the stars and the starlight and we know that it is the stars that give the morning dew. Even if there is no rain, the plants and animals will still have water. And so too we know that it is the starlight that has provided direction to us so that we will not get lost. The stars will help us to know when to plant and when to have our ceremonies. And so to all of the stars we put our minds together as one mind and extend a greeting and thanksgiving to the stars.

And so too, there are the ones responsible for bringing us the good news telling us how to go about and carry on in this world. It is these who have tried to help us to understand where we are and to carry ourselves in this creation and so, to these beings, the messengers of the Creator, we put our minds together as one mind and extend a greeting and a thanksgiving.

And now there is the Creator, the great mystery. It is the creator that brought us all of these things and we know that all that is necessary for life and happiness is provided for us. And it is true, also, that no one will know the creator's face as we travel about on this earth but that the creator simply asks us to greet one another and be thankful and grateful to all that we see about us for they are the ones who give us life. And so as we gather here we put our minds together as one mind and extend a greeting and thanksgiving to our Creator.

And now, if there is anything that has been left out and the people listening have remembered a special thing that should receive a greeting and a thanksgiving, it should be remembered that we have not learned all to which we are to give greetings; other times we are forgetful. If there are things that have been left out, now is the time to extend a special greeting and thanksgiving.

organization would publish a booklet called *Are We Giving America Back to the Indians?* Distributed by the Interstate Congress for Equal Rights and Responsibilities, this organization argued that all remaining Indian-owned land and resources should be nationalized for the use of all Americans.[5] In 1988, Jack Weatherford published his book, *Indian Givers*, demonstrating how the Indians of the Americas transformed the world by giving their gifts of food, medicine, agriculture, architecture, urban planning and government.[6]

Today, giveaway ceremonies are held throughout the United States. In the Pacific Northwest, these practices are known as Potlatches. At times of celebrations, of personal achievements or of death, families would hold a giveaway (Potlatch) to commemorate the special event and to provide a feast for the tribe, giving away some of their cherished possessions to all who attended. Sometimes, simple household utensils would be given away. At other times, expensive blankets and handmade items would be shared. In many cases, Indian nation leadership was determined by how often an individual gave away everything he or she owned for the sake of the larger community.

In the early years and sometimes today, giveaway or Potlatch ceremonies of the various Native nations enabled families to have enough food and clothing for the hard winters. Tribal leaders were responsible for the equitable distribution of these goods to the people. While these ceremonies continue to have an important cultural place in the lives of more traditional Indians, it has only been since the middle of the twentieth century that laws forbidding giveaway practices and other traditional observances have been set aside by the federal government and a variety of states. The original laws prohibiting these practices perhaps demonstrated a fear of their power, a recognition that they were part of the fabric of Indian civilization and a source of tribal health.

Spirituality: The Highest Form of Political Consciousness

Historian Robert Berkhofer teaches that "American Indian history must move from being primarily a record of white-Indian relations to become the story of Indians in the United States (or North America) over time."[9] It is difficult to separate the two. Each is inextricably bound to the other. However, this record becomes the story of Indians today because they are the ones who remember the narratives and attempt to live in the context of this history, struggling to secure their cultural and racial survival. The stories are passed from generation to generation through the elders and through oral histories. They have shaped the lives, destinies and programs of tribal (nation) entities to this very day. The relationships between the immigrant populations and America's Native people often seem ponderous and redundant because events throughout history seem to repeat themselves and rarely evolve to reach solutions satisfactory to either group.

"The traditional Native peoples hold the key to the reversal of the processes in Western Civilization which holds the promise of unimaginable future suffering and destruction. Spiritualism is the highest form of political consciousness. And we, the Native peoples of the Western Hemisphere, are among the world's surviving proprietors of that kind of consciousness..."[7]

THE POMO SACRED BASKET

When persons travel from one culture to observe the patterns of another culture, they often find it difficult to reconcile what they feel and experience with what their culture has taught them. The construction of the California Pomo Indian basket is one of the many stories that illustrate an ageless practice threatened by cultural upheaval and social interference. The construction of the Pomo basket is a story nearly lost to history but one that is instructive in understanding traditional Native cultural practices. The Pomi Chitu, or sacred basket, has an important place in the moral and cultural development of Pomo children and provides an example of an ancient cultural phenomenon that has been eroded over the years by the forces of Western value systems and the inability of the immigrant culture to understand its place in Native society. To explain the basket is to explain the culture itself.

These water-tight, bright-plumed baskets provided an education for young girls that could not be obtained in any other manner. Working with willow, pine root, cedar root, redbud, feathers and other materials, the California Pomo Indian woman produced what archeologists and anthropologists have described as the finest baskets made by any people in the world. The European observers noted the method of construction and commented on the brilliance of the plumes and the complexity of the patterns. Many of the descriptions were recorded as a scientific measure designed to freeze in the memory of history this wonderful craft and the women who made them. But in their documentation, they were never able to capture the essence of Pomo basketry.

"The whites, too, shall pass—perhaps sooner than other tribes. Continue to contaminate your bed, and you will one night suffocate in your own waste. When the buffalo are all slaughtered, the wild horses all tamed, the secret corners of the forest heavy with the scent of many men, and the view of the ripe hills blotted by talking wires, where is the thicket? Gone. Where is the eagle? Gone. And what is it to say goodbye to the swift and the hunt, the end of living and the beginning of survival?"[8]

The Pomo creation story recites the beginning of the people who came to earth in a basket. The infant girl lives in a basket that is probably the same one used by her mother and grandmother. For an Indian girl to learn how to weave a basket is to learn about the whole world. First, she learned the differences between plants. Some were used for baskets, others for food and medicine. As she learned about food plants, she also learned the use of baskets to prepare food. Because it took close to a year to gather the materials for the construction of the basket, the young girl learned about the seasons and her place in relation to her family, her tribe, other people and the natural world.

Perhaps the most important lesson is that the earth is Mother of us all. From her come the materials for the basket hat that the young girl wears representing her femaleness. Her grandmother and grandfather are her teachers while her parents supply her physical needs as she learns. To learn how to make a basket is to understand how to behave. Plants must be gathered promptly to coincide with life's cycles. Gentleness must be employed in preparing the plants for weaving. Patience is exercised to assure that each strand is in its place. A task begun must be continued to its completion. A partially finished basket or a poorly made one will serve no purpose. And so, from large baskets to small ones, from fat ones to flat ones, from baskets used every day to those used only on special occasions, the young Indian girl learns about life from the time she is born until she is a very old woman.[10]

The Pomo Indian story can be repeated time and time again about other Indian cultures and nations. Over and over, traditional practices were supplanted by Western values and the roles of women and children shifted to majority culture models forcing the abandonment of ancient teachings and wisdom. Each time the change would leave its own images of pathos. History records days, years and centuries of the European/Christian settlement of the Americas and the subsequent collection of reports, artifacts and bones that were stored in archives and museums. These relics were gathered by anthropologists and ethnologists who, like the culture to which they belong, needed to preserve the history of the "children of the forest," the "Noble Savage," the original American. There seemed to be little care taken for the survival of the cultures themselves, for the cultures proved to be obstacles to the spread of "civilization" and the quest for land and riches. The church and its missions played a major role in this process, which moved writer Adam Smith to observe that the pious purpose of converting Indians to Christianity was to sanctify the injustice of colonization and economic development.

The Virginia and Massachusetts settlements at the beginning of the seventeenth century are generally regarded by Western historians as the beginning of the North American colonial period. Grade school children still learn stories about Captain John Smith and the first Thanksgiving as a means of imparting knowledge about America's European settlers. Glossed over are the political and economic motives driving these immigrants: their heavy indebtedness to creditors in London and elsewhere that pressed them to develop a trade economy. This fact compromised their quest for religious freedom–often cited as their primary motive for immigration to the Americas–and tied them to their hunger for land and wealth. A Seneca chief would observe two hundred years later that the Native people willingly gave the immigrants a place to live, but the settlers were not satisfied until they acquired a larger and larger space leaving the Indian with no place to spread a blanket.[11]

An Onondaga chief often recites today a litany of conscience: Once upon a time, the skies would be clouded for hours with flocks of passenger pigeons. Where did they go and who took them away? Once the plains were filled with Buffalo who would take days to pass by. Where did they go and who took them away? Once there were, perhaps, 100 millions of Native peoples in North and Central American. Where did they go and who took them away?[12]. The census of Native peoples in the Americas at the time of Columbus' arrival has always been a point of sharp contention among scholars. Some say that the number of Native people in the United States today equals those at the time of "discovery." The 2000 census figures show Native populations in the United States at about four million.[13] However, the Newberry Library Center for the History of the American Indian has examined a stream of sources, including early Spanish enumerations, and places the number as high as 100 million at the time of Columbus' arrival.[14]

EARLY EXPLORATION

The very early history of exploration and "discovery" by European or Asian venturers is shrouded in mystery. Apart from legends embedded in Native storytelling, there is scant documentation for modern historians to point to the explorer, the time or the place of contact with the American continent or its people. We begin to learn more about the wild possibilities as we hear about the Viking landing on the tip of Cape Cod in the year 1000. There, as research has confirmed, the Vikings established a temporary settlement and soon thereafter departed, carrying Native people into slavery. It is believed that the Vatican Archives could yield significant insight into these early explorations.

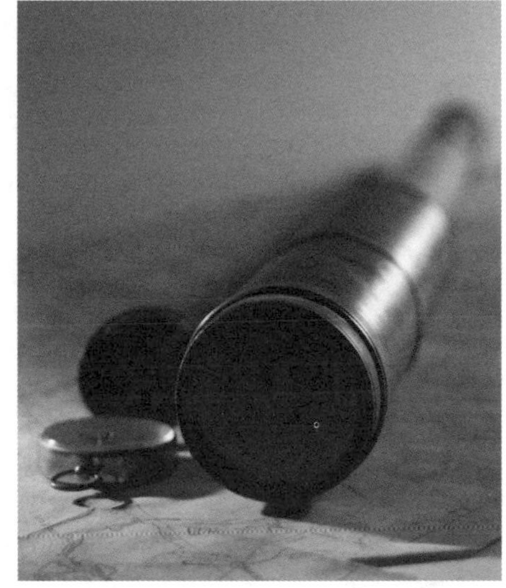

De Soto

In 1538, Hernando de Soto led military forces on behalf of Spain through Florida and other territories in the southeastern area of what became the United States searching for the fountain of youth and riches for his country. His tactics were violent and cruel, pitting military forces against people unprepared for such imbalances in weaponry and inhuman motivations. De Soto intended to establish a colony and brought with him a score of priests and such craftsmen and skilled artisans as would contribute to the establishment of European-styled settlements. His large supply of horses proved to be formidable in the conquest. In violent assaults on Native peoples, many of those horses escaped to begin the first herds of mustangs in Western North America. De Soto's violent incursions established no permanent settlements and literally decimated the Native nations in whose territories he traveled. Cherokee, Choctaw, Chickasaws, and a huge array of other Indian tribes fell victim to his lust for riches, particularly gold. The rare engravings executed by Theodore DeBray, the expedition's artist, demonstrate the violence of de Soto toward the Native populations.

By this time, Spanish incursions into Central and South American were well underway. In 1541, the Spanish Council of the Indies met to adjudicate the human nature of the Indians of the Americas. If Indians were considered beasts of burden, they would be assigned to the control of the military. If they had souls, they would fall under the tutelage of the church. Both criteria promoted the exploitation of American Indians as inferior beings and led to outrageous assaults on their populations.

THE LOST COLONY OF ROANOKE AND JAMESTOWN

The next European immigrations would prove to be more successful in establishing a foothold in the "new world." One such foray in 1584, though short-lived, produced the first English colony in North America on Roanoke Island off the coast of what is now North Carolina. Sir Walter Raleigh had secured a charter to establish such a colony from Queen Elizabeth I. By the end of 1587, the colony no longer existed. Relief ships returning from England found no trace of the settlers lodged there in previous years. There is strong evidence to suggest that the remnant English colonists had assimilated with local Native people, for when the last relief ships landed on the Outer Banks of North Carolina, there were few physical remains of the colonists. However, it has been reported in some of the narratives that Native people were observed engaging in Christian practices.

Lumbee Indian scholars and others have provided important documentation reinforcing their belief that this history forms the origin stories of the Lumbee people. One such teacher/scholar was Adolph Dial, well-known United Methodist Lumbee from

North Carolina. Although there is great conjecture around the origin of the Lumbee peoples, they themselves nurture a tribal history connecting them to the "lost colony." Today the Lumbees comprise one of two of the largest United Methodist Native populations in the United States.

A failed or lost colony or not, the Roanoke venture marked a new era of exploration and immigration from Europe. The next wave of North American colonization came to Jamestown, Virginia in 1607, established by the London Company of Virginia, and was considerably more tenacious.

PLYMOUTH COLONY

Perhaps motivated by the successful Jamestown settlement, the best known and one of the most thoroughly studied colonization projects came about when the Mayflower and its passengers entered Cape Cod harbor on November 11, 1620. Their original destination was somewhere around Hudson Bay, then thought to be part of Virginia. Although Native people had seen fishing boats before and it is reasonable to believe that they had contact with the sailors, this ship and its occupants would have a lasting impact on the Native populations and the continent that would become the United States.

...the Roanoke venture marked a new era of exploration and immigration from Europe.

The first European child born in New England took breath on board the Mayflower in Cape Cod Bay. Upon their arrival, an exploratory party was sent out to find fresh water and food. Miles Standish led the search, traveling south and east and arriving at a place now known as Corn Hill. There Standish and his crew discovered a cache of corn and carried it back to the Mayflower. Later, this theft of Pamet Indian seed corn would figure into one of the first treaties between the immigrant population and Native people.

Pressing on to the mainland, the Puritans, or Pilgrims or Separatists, as they preferred to think of themselves, established a settlement in an abandoned Native village. Later named Plymouth Colony by the new settlers (suggested by Captain John Smith), this new enterprise would come to shape the lives, destiny and governments of Native people throughout America and eventually give birth to a republic as the colonies consolidated their social and political organizations.

Contact with the resident population occurred very soon as the new arrivals faced hardships in providing themselves with enough food and adequate shelter to survive. The Wampanoags, the Native nation in whose land they had settled, played a key role in the survival of these Pilgrims and taught them lessons in diplomacy and treaty-making as well. Massasoit, the powerful Wampanoag leader, would include in his first agreement with the Pilgrims the theft of the Pamet seed corn as part of a code of behavior as relationships were more formally negotiated and agreed upon. In this agreement, Massasoit insisted that if the colonists had the capacity to steal from Indians and trespass against them, they had the capacity to violate Native people again.

The Pilgrims had signed their "Mayflower Compact" aboard the Mayflower upon their arrival in Cape Cod Bay. That document established a civil government with majority decision-making and declared loyalty to the king. These rudiments of civil law did not take into consideration relationships with or the culture and practices of America's Native people. Development and codification of rules and laws would evolve as various colonies were formed and unified governance was perfected to keep order and establish authority.

Somewhat later, the Charter of Massachusetts charged the

governor and company to "...wynn and incite the Natives...(to) the onlie true God and Saviour of Mankinde." Up and down the east coast of America, the newly arrived settlers were at odds with Indians who appeared to be worshiping many "gods." They much preferred to worship the Father, Son and Holy Ghost. It was clear that the Indians revered and cared for the water, land, mountains, animals and various life forms. The colonists could not grasp the fact that these entities were "gods" for Native people. They belonged to the Great Spirit, the Great Mystery. This Native theology would perplex the colonial generations just as much as it would their descendants living three hundred years later.

The Pilgrims asked the Indians for nothing short of full church participation. This expectation had serious consequences for Native cultures since it required reading the Bible in English and demanded social and cultural conversion before total religious conversion could be achieved. In time, missionaries such as John Eliot would begin to bring the Word to the Indians in their own language. The missionary effort, in both its early and later stages, usually resulted in the establishment of schools, European-style government and the use of European clothes and tools. Still, the converts were very few as were the numbers of immigrants attempting to win their souls. So few, in fact, were the immigrants in both Massachusetts and Virginia that the English monarchs moved carefully in the early stages of settlement because of the imbalance of strength in the Indians' favor.

King Charles II, in his 1677 treaty with the Virginia Indians, called them Indian Kings and Queens and proceeded to guarantee Indian property rights "forever." Perhaps this explains at least one origin of the modern usage of Indian "princess," attributing royalty lines to Native leaders that never before existed. Charles

II's treaty also guaranteed the restraining of colonists from settling or farming within three miles of any Native lands. It is important to remember that at this time immigrants were still outnumbered and treaded lightly on the manners, customs and culture of the Native residents. Although this did not always hold true, it generally characterized the behavior of the settlers until they gained sufficient numbers to shoulder military defenses. They then carried out the Europeanizing and Christianizing campaigns that would become so destructive to the unity of Indian civilization. And then the tables turned, spurred by the availability of tobacco in Virginia, to be sold as a cash crop in order to satisfy creditors in Europe. Population pressures in New England and the hunger to expand their land base also contributed to the change.

NATIVE RELIGION AND GOVERNMENT

Indians were never thought by any European measure to be civilized. After all, they were seen as being nomadic. They had no art galleries, libraries or museums. They produced no great paintings on canvas or board. They had no universities. The colonists could not understand cultures that were not based on materialistic models. Native people had always existed in the Americas. Ask any traditional Indian elder today—whether on the plains or in the mountains or forests or deserts—where we came from and they will tell you "We have always been here." Even James Michener in his book *Alaska*, written in the 1980s, deferred to European explanations of the origin of Native people in North America. He characterized them as having traveled from Asia across the great land bridge to what is now Alaska, then immigrating south to populate the Americas.[15] Of course, this theory is debunked by traditional Indian creation and origin stories, but is still the theory dominantly espoused by today's historians and anthropologists.

Native Americans had complicated faith systems, tribal laws, sophisticated trade routes and clearly articulated social systems that often cast women in primary authority and leadership roles. In the context of spiritual understandings of who they were, Native Americans practiced ritual hunting ceremonies and even ritual war ceremonies preparing themselves for the hunt or the battle They understood themselves as sovereign people and exercised cultural freedom and political autonomy throughout all of their tribal/nation organizations. Native peoples never claimed ownership of land. Mother Earth could not be owned. It was to be shared and cared for by the people. Their governments were often highly refined and, as the colonial enterprises moved toward the founding of a republic known as the United States of America, they were instructive in the formation of a new Bill of Rights and a Constitution that would count them as mere savages.

...the immigrants immediately set about proving that these life forces of creation were not sacred by despoiling, colonizing and eliminating them

Since the beginning of immigration to North America, Christians have told Native people that Christians have a superior or "correct" understanding of God. They believed that Native people worshiped the things of creation and told them that the mountains were not sacred, nor were the streams, the forests, the birds, the animals or the plants. Though a harsh observation, the immigrants immediately set about proving that these life forces of creation were not sacred by despoiling, colonizing and eliminating them. Is it any wonder that we are currently faced with such environmental emergencies?

Our oral histories and stories teach us lessons poignantly valuable today as we attempt to understand ourselves in the twenty-first century. We were told in the creator's original

The elders say that the soil is rich from the bones of thousands of generations.

instructions that we have been provided with all the things necessary for life. We were instructed to show great respect for all of the beings of the earth. We were taught that our life exists beside the Tree of life and that our well-being depends on the well being of the Vegetable life. We are close relatives of the four-legged beings. Because we honor all of life, living things belong to our spiritual universe. The Creator enters into and sustains the acts of creation. The spiritual universe, then, embraces the creation that produces and sustains life. We are a part of that creation and our duty is to support life in its relationship with all living beings.

In the teachings of the elders from the Longhouse (Haudenosaunee), of the Six Nations Iroquois, we learn that human beings are to walk about on the earth in a manner that expresses great respect, with affection and gratitude toward all of the manifestations of the Creator. We give a greeting and offer thanksgiving to the many supporters of our lives–corn, beans, squash, the winds, the water, the sun, all living beings who work together on this land. When people cease to respect and express gratitude for these things, all of life will be destroyed and human life as we know it on this planet will come to an end.

Our roots are deep in the lands where we live. The elders say that the soil is rich from the bones of thousands of generations. All of us were created in these territories and on these lands. It is our duty to take great care of them because from these lands will spring the future generations. Caring for the earth is not a project of the Sierra Club or other environmental organizations, it is a way of life.[16]

SOVEREIGNTY AND MANIFEST DESTINY

To this very day, the issues of sovereignty have plagued both the Native inhabitants of America and the newcomers. Then as today, the right of Native people to exercise complete power over their geographical homelands was questioned. Indians had always exercised sovereignty over their territories. Violent encounters with other Native nations and entities as well as westward-moving European settlers, for the most part, grew out of an understanding of tribal/nation sovereignty and territorial rights. Incidents of national aggression–that is, aggression against Native nations by other Native groups or by colonial or federal powers—was met with measures of rigorous defense.

The new immigrants embraced concepts of sovereignty not shared by Indian nations. Images of Manifest Destiny gave tone, texture and context to European concepts of sovereignty that allowed them to interfere in the affairs of other nations. Originally understood as the inherent right and ultimate good to expand the principle ideals of the dominant culture–in this case the Anglo Saxon race—the spirit of Manifest Destiny found its fullest expression in America by claiming land and dominance from the east coast to the west coast of what is now the continental United States. Though a phrase not common until the nineteenth century, the meaning and power of its sentiments took root at the beginning of the colonial era. Manifest Destiny was founded upon racial superiority and a compulsion to make manifest the destiny of the immigrant population and a value system alien to the civilizations into whose territories the new settlers migrated.

Images of Manifest Destiny gave tone, texture and context to European concepts of sovereignty that allowed them to interfere in the affairs of other nations.

Probably the finest definition of Manifest Destiny was provided, perhaps unwittingly, by Robert Frost, when he recited his poem "The Gift Outright" at the inauguration of President John F. Kennedy. The poignant line, "...The land was ours before we were the land's..." captures the essence of Manifest Destiny in a way no scholar or historian has been able to articulate quite so clearly. The immigrants to the North American continent surely believed that the land was theirs long before they set eyes upon it. This philosophy and the ensuing struggle to vanquish the land and its people brought Native Americans to their current state of emergency.

Legal scholar of Indian law and history Felix Cohen said that Indians were the miner's canaries of American society. The multiple ills that are visited upon them are only a prelude and a harbinger of what is to be expected for society as a whole. We see this prophecy coming to fruition today as the original immigrant values systems have taken shape in social, political and economic policies. While we will later examine a few of the specifics of these implications, we must follow the story as it continued from colonial times.

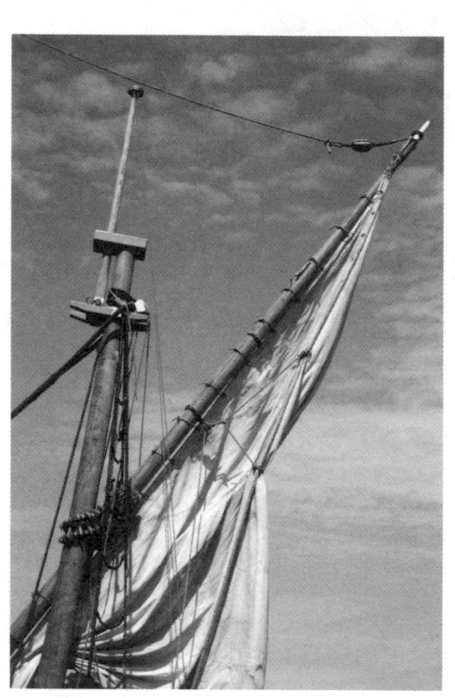

"...The land was ours before we were the land's..."
—Robert Frost

CIVILIZING INDIANS

Christian European values strove for dominance, holding Native cultures in contempt, fearing the warrior and undermining the role of women in the various Native societies. These notions were expressed in an effort to turn Indians into New England farmers, thereby changing the patterns of tribal lifestyle. The underlying assumption was an insistence that farming was to be valued more highly than hunting and fishing. In many cultures, this meant the displacement of Indian women as the men became farmers. European-styled agricultural communities best served the purposes of civilization, for the clearing of land, the planting of crops and the construction of small villages would bring stability and control.

Control, indeed, would lead to "civilized" stability. Tribal communal agricultural lands were converted into individual allocations, introducing the concept of the private ownership of land. This was contradictory to Indian belief and practice and undermined traditional Native systems (the fullest impact of this practice would be felt in the General Allotment Act of 1887 that will be dealt with in a later chapter). The imposition of new regulations and control measures became more complex as private ownership of property gave birth to "protective" laws. New legal protections led to systems of guarding private property that in turn spawned complex enforcement and punishment systems totally alien to the Native experience. One can picture colonial "no trespassing" signs, police arrests, new courts, jails and the English jury system.

Native people had always managed their own legal systems for dealing with societal violations such as murder, theft and other infractions. Now, matters that would have been dealt with in the old traditional tribal manner and in a much more civil way were handled by imprisonment. Among Jesuit mission practices in North America, even flogging and chaining to enforce "holy lifestyles" became acceptable treatment of the unsaved "savage." [17] Theoretically, once all of these new measures were in place and Indians were brought to the Cross, industriousness and the desire to have, own and acquire would have ushered in the Christian reformation of Native people. But in spite of these radical changes upon the land and among its original people, the colonial period could be described as manifestly humanitarian as compared to the Federal period that would soon follow.

CHAPTER 2

The Battle to Capture the Hearts and Minds of Indian Nations

Immigrants and their God have been in contention with Native faith systems for more than five hundred years. As we shall see, both church and government would repeat its efforts to capture the loyalties of American Indians by asserting their superiority and instituting control measures that would hobble and then crush the original inhabitants. After a period of time when the boundaries between European colonial society and Native societies were more illusive, the birth of the British Missionary Society in London in 1795 zealously renewed this project. America was preoccupied with nationhood, the American Revolution and the quest for liberty as expressed in the Bill of Rights, the Declaration of Independence and the Constitution of the United States.

This new mission society appealed to the "...serious and zealous professors of the Gospel of every denomination respecting an attempt to evangelize the heathen."[18] In spite of their declaration to "...utterly and sincerely disclaim all political views and party design; abhorring all attempts to disturb order and government... vigorously united...sending ministers of Christ to preach the Gospel among the heathen..."[19], missionaries and their churches would soon be entering into collusive relationships with governments to achieve mutually agreeable goals for the subjugation of indigenous populations. At the time this challenge was issued to evangelize the pagan areas of the world, the mission society estimated that there were 481 millions of pagans, destitute of the knowledge of the true God and Jesus Christ. Thus reinvigorated, the mission enterprise was staged to play a decisive role in the historical drama about to commence.

THE ALBANY PLAN OF UNION

For the previous forty years before this new mission initiative, colonial powers and Indian nations were uneasily attempting to co-exist. Indians saw the growing European population as a direct threat to their remaining territories. Unjust deals were still the order of the day in negotiations between the colonists and the tribes. But in 1754, the organized colonies met in Fort Orange, now Albany, New York, to negotiate alliances and agreements with Indian nations. They also sought to devise their own means of collaborating with each other as they developed documents of unity and governance while preparing for increasing threats from the French to the north.

Benjamin Franklin was among the representatives of seven British North American colonies meeting in this Albany Congress. It was he who produced what would be called the "Albany Plan of Union." Although rejected by the legislatures of seven colonies (not to mention the king), this plan of union was later adapted to create the Articles of Confederation leading to the writing of the United States Constitution. There is strong reason to believe that Native governments contributed to the formation of the founding documents of United States independence–especially the Iroquois or Haudenosaunee, who were among the conferees in the Albany Congress and were doubtless questioned about their forms of government.

It is clear from the historical records that colonial peoples–both official representatives and ordinary citizens–had more than a casual understanding of Indian lifestyles and the liberty and equality they represented. Native governments generally demonstrated this understanding in their forms of governance and social practices. In the late 1600's, a French baron, reporting in an account of his American years, could not understand why

> "...one Man should have more than another, and that the Rich should have more Respect than the Poor...They brand us for Slaves, and call us miserable Souls, whose life is not worth having, alleging, That we degrade ourselves in subjecting our selves to one Man [a king] who possesses the whole Power, and is bound by no Law but his own Will... [Individual Indians] value themselves above anything that you can imagine, and this is the reason they always give for't, *That one's as much Master as another, and since Men are all made of the same Clay there should be no Distinction or Superiority among them.* {Emphasis in original.}"[20]

TWO ROW WAMPUM AGREEMENT

Familiar to most northeastern colonists was the two row wampum agreement of the Six Nations Iroquois (Haudenosaunee) with the early seventeenth century Dutch settlers. The wampum belt was woven with two parallel rows of purple seashell beads surrounded by three rows of white beads. Sometimes called the two canoe wampum treaty, this belt represented an understanding that the Haudenosaunee and the colonists would live in two separate boats–the Indian canoe and the colonists' ships–in mutual harmony but with individual autonomy and freedom to conduct their own affairs according to the dictates and regulations devised by each. The two row wampum belt was repeatedly presented to succeeding generations and re-affirmed as a standard for international relations. Even George Washington held the wampum belt in conversations with the Haudenosaunee and today it is occasionally brought into the Longhouse of the Iroquois as a reminder of peace and friendship between two societies.

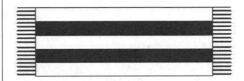

The wampum belt was woven with two parallel rows of purple seashell beads surrounded by three rows of white beads.

THE GREAT LAW OF PEACE

The story did not begin there, however. It started with the original Five Nations of the Haudenosaunee and the advent of the Great Law of Peace. The sixth nation, the Tuscarora, would join the Iroquois confederacy sometime in the early 1700s. In the early second century when the original Five Nations and other Native nations were constantly at war with one another, there appeared from the north a prophet named Deganawidah, the Peacemaker. It is said that he was born to a virgin woman and, as a grown man, came to the Haudenosaunee traveling in a stone canoe. Deganawidah brought a message of peace. But because he had a speech impediment he was limited in sharing his message with the people. He linked up with Ayenwatha (made famous by Henry Wadsworth Longfellow's misguided poem "Hiawatha"), an orator from the Onondaga Nation. Over a long period of time, together they succeeded in stitching together an alliance among the Mohawk, Seneca, Cayuga and Oneida Nations. The fifth nation, the Onondaga with their leader the Tododaho, resisted joining this amalgam of nations. "In a parley, Deganawidah took a single arrow and invited Tododaho to break it, which he did easily. Then he bundled together five arrows and asked Tododaho to break the lot. He was unable to do so. In the same way, Deganawidah prophesied, the Five Nations, each weak on its own, would fall into darkness unless they all banded together."[21] Soon the Tododaho agreed upon the alliance.

Together, the Five Nations of the Haudenosaunee agreed on a constitution known as the Great Law of Peace. They established the limits of the new Grand Council, agreeing that they would govern relationships among the Five Nations and outside entities, but that affairs internal to each nation would be handled by them individually. The council negotiated peace treaties but declarations of war were left to the individual member nations of the confederacy. When issues were to be decided among the Five Nations, the Tododaho–who by agreement was the chief of chiefs–would send out runners to announce to member nations the gathering of the Grand Council. The selected representatives or chiefs of the different nations gathered to make the decisions that were required to be unanimous.

Consensus was the manner in which decisions were made and it is still employed today in all deliberations of the Grand Council. This was a true consensus process, little resembling what we call consensus making today. One of the many unique features of the consensus decision-making process was that all decisions were required to take into account the impact of their final choices on the next seven generations.[22] Today the Six Nations Haudenosaunee is the longest-surviving democracy in the world and their unique passports are recognized by many nations.

...all decisions were required to take into account the impact of the final choices on the next seven generations.

While there is common agreement among Native peoples about the contributions of Native thought and governmental organization to the founding documents of a new nation, there are many scholars who disagree. In any case, while Native organization and social practices may have prepared a new nation to order its life in legal constitutional ways (as Charles Mann points out in 1491), Native Americans would not celebrate the behavior of the new federal government that superseded state law or its dependence on majority rule instead of consensus. Nor would they celebrate its tolerance of discrimination against women, African Americans, Indians or other dispossessed peoples. Finally, of course, Indians would not be pleased with the Constitution's emphasis on private property and the heightened emphasis on the importance of the individual at the expense of communal values.[23]

When the Constitution of the United States was ratified in 1789, Blacks were considered 3/5ths human and American Indians were still savages. Of particular note for our discussions is the reference to Article VI, Section 2, of the Constitution guaranteeing that all treaties made between the United States and other entities are the law of the land. This article would be violated almost from its inception by the United States. During the treaty-making period between 1776 and 1871, the United States entered into well over four hundred treaties with Native American tribes and nations. While forests have been cleared to supply paper for books covering the American Revolution and the founding of the new republic, we will spend little time on this phase of history. Our focus will be on the behavior of the new nation and the role Christian churches played in the unfolding panorama of Native American survival.

BEGINNINGS OF METHODISM IN AMERICA

Because of its eighteenth century origins, Methodism got a late start in America. It wasn't until John Wesley became a parish priest in Savannah, Georgia, in 1735 that Indians became an object of ministry for the founder of Methodism. Wesley, failing to establish any outreach to Native people, returned home to England rebuffed and disappointed. Upon his arrival in America in 1771, Francis Asbury ordained David Avery as a missionary to the Oneida Nation. In 1784, appointed by Wesley as the superintendent of American Methodism, Thomas Coke, known as the father of Methodist mission, devised a plan for The Society for the Establishment of Missions Among the Heathen. In 1786, just two years before the ratification of the United States Constitution, Methodist missions among the "heathen" began.

The "Civilizing" Process

The mission efforts among Christian churches would introduce European institutions as a means of enhancing the "civilizing" process among Native people. The insistence of European forms of church, home, school, marriage and the education of children at distances from parents served to shatter age-old Native practices and customs. As an inducement to join the civilizing process, certain economic or trade privileges were often granted Christian Indians to attract poor, traditional Indians. Control measures were employed by the missions to discourage traditional Indian culture and political practices. These were replaced with Western models of authority, thereby introducing extraordinary conflicts among Indian people never before experienced in their traditions. Confusion, conflict and divisiveness abounded as old ways of dealing with marriage and the social aspects of cultural life were compromised by Christian principles that defied traditional Indian values. The eighteenth-century religious revival known as the Great Awakening would continue to wield its influence into the nineteenth century.

THE FRIENDS' SURVEY

The proofs of being "civilized" and having accepted the Gospel of Jesus Christ as understood by European settlers and their missionaries were to be demonstrated by Indians in farming, in changed diets, and in the adoption of homespun clothing, shoes, clipped hair and a new philosophy embracing private ownership of property. This ideology represented a "new world" mode of operation that shaped the federal/church relationships with Native people into the twenty-first century. This nationalistic philosophy is perhaps best encapsulated in a report commissioned by the Society of Friends in New York,

It has been suggested that the term "cram it down your throat" derived from this meeting with Missionary Cram.

The Commentary of Red Jacket

Perhaps one of the most lucid commentaries on the relationship of Christian missions to Native people came from an old Seneca chief in 1805. Missionary Cram was sent to Red Jacket and others of the principal chiefs and warriors at Buffalo Creek (now Buffalo, New York) to instruct the Indians on "how to worship the Great Spirit." Red Jacket was acquainted with the Christian church and knew that while nomadic Hebrews were eulogized, transient Indians needed to be "civilized." Christians talked about the Holy Ghost in their places of worship while at the same time damning the Indian spirit world. Red Jacket had witnessed denominations reluctant to share pulpits, yet proclaiming the unifying nature of God's Word. It was out of this context that the chief replied to Mr. Cram after patiently listening to him deliver his message:

> "Brother, our seats were once large and yours were small. You have now become a great people, and we have scarcely a place left to spread our blankets. You have got our country but are not satisfied; you want to force your religion upon us...You say that you are sent to instruct us how to worship the Great Spirit agreeably to his mind, and if we do not take hold of the religion which you white people teach, we shall be unhappy hereafter... We understand that your religion is written in a book. If it was intended for us as well as you, why has not the Great Spirit given it to us, and not only to us, but why did he not give to our forefathers the knowledge of that book with the means of understanding it rightly? We only know what you tell us about it. How shall we know what to believe, being so often deceived by the white people? Brother, you say there is but one way to worship and serve the Great Spirit. If there is but one religion why do you white people differ so much about it? Why not all agree, as you can all read the book?... Brother, we are told that you have been preaching to white people in this place. These people are our neighbors, we are acquainted with them. We will wait a little while and see what effect your preaching has upon them. If we find it does them good, makes them honest and less disposed to cheat Indians, we will then consider again what you have said..."[24]

Philadelphia and Baltimore–with the blessing of the U. S. House of Representatives–regarding the condition of the "sons of the forest" in what was then the Western frontier at the close of the War of 1812. It was in their interest to prove that under a judicious system of care and protection, the Natives of the continent could not only be greatly improved in their conditions but induced to abandon their wandering and savage mode of life for the more rational one of local habitation and agricultural pursuit so peacefully enjoyed by their more enlightened neighbors. The justification for this commissioned survey was the prevention of Natives from becoming extinct "at a distant period" due to their "suffering situation."

Under these circumstances and with a stated expression of "charity and benevolence" the Friends appointed committees and commenced to survey the Indian nations with the conviction that the interests of the Indians would be promoted and preserved "by abandoning the chase for the plough and the farm, the tomahawk and scaling knife for the wholesome restraints of civil law and the misconceptions of their benighted superstitions for the truths unfolded by the lights of the Gospel."[25] The survey went on to cite the most important signs of civilizing influences by enumerating how much land was under cultivation; the number of livestock, including hogs, cattle, horses, sheep, cows and oxen; numbers of grist mills, saw mills, frame houses, barns, ploughs, sleds, carts, wagons, carpenters, blacksmiths, shoemakers, tailors and weavers; and the annual production of linen and woolen cloth. The Friends believed that by the extension of suitable protection and care on the part of the government, the "Native sons" might be brought within the pale of civilization and become incorporated with the "American people."

The Friends believed that by extension of suitable protection and care on the part of the government, "Native sons" might be brought within the pale of civilization...

The report concluded with the hope that under a humane and

pacific policy by the government carried out by the system of laws, the Indians could be dissuaded of their migratory habits and find sufficient interest in property to settle in "fixed habitation." Further, under a system of laws and domestic discipline, Indians could be improved in well-regulated schools to enable them to become competitors with their white brethren for the rewards of excellence, virtue and knowledge. While attempting to provide assistance to Native people, the Friends were to open doors used by the government to extinguish a people.

THE FIVE CIVILIZED TRIBES

Perhaps no Indian nations were more rapidly educated and assimilated than the Five Nations in the south whose cultural and economic achievements earned them the title of the "Five Civilized Tribes." These tribes were the Cherokee, Chickasaw, Choctaw, Creek and Seminole. The first four had adopted governments similar to those of the states and all of them lived very much as their white neighbors. Yet President Andrew Jackson's inaugurated removal policies that attempted to transfer all Native peoples to the west beyond the Mississippi River–including the five tribes who by now reflected the "best" characteristics of civilization.

Treaty-Making and Breaking

Before returning to this story, we must remember that the treaty-making process exercised by the new republic extended from 1776 until 1871, during which time the United States and Indian nations entered into well over four hundred legal agreements that were recognized as covenants between sovereign nation powers according to the Constitution, Article VI, Section 2. Treaty rights and the legal and political status of Indians and their relationship to states and the federal government have remained issues of controversy to this day. The Indian nations have always regarded these legal agreements as sacred covenants even though the United States was to deny or break all of them. While this writer worked on the American Indian Policy Review Commission from 1975 to1976, it was the official position of the Congress of the United States that all Indian treaties were intact except those that were changed by Congress or otherwise abrogated. Until twenty years ago, the Supreme Court of the United States favored the Indian understanding of law and the judgements and rulings of the court generally reflected Native legal interpretations. We shall later see what impact this change has had on Native issues.

The Removal Bill

Andrew Jackson brought about one of the earliest and bloodiest assaults on these treaties and the people with whom they were made when he cooperated with the southern states in the forcible removal of their Native inhabitants. These Five Civilized Tribes occupied territory badly needed by a new culture whose expanding population with its agricultural and industrial needs–not to mention the greed born out of the discovery of gold–hungered for space to grow. In a message to Congress on December 6, 1830, Jackson articulated a policy of extinguishing all Indian title to eastern Indian lands and pushing the inhabitants of those lands to territories west of the Mississippi. He said that the action would open to "dense and civilized population(s)" areas formerly occupied only by "a few savage hunters."

These Five Nations had all made great advancement in the arts of white civilizations. The Cherokees perhaps best epitomized this progress having established the publication of a newspaper in 1828 using an alphabet invented by Sequoia. They lived in frame houses, engaged in animal husbandry and even had glass or isinglass in their windows. In spite of these signs of domestication, many Indian tribes would be removed to the new "Indian Territory." Any person who sought to influence others not to emigrate to the west would be imprisoned. The governor of Georgia wrote to all missionaries notifying them that they would be arrested if they did not leave the state. The Removal Bill was passed by Congress on May 28, 1831. Protesting the act, several missionaries, including two Methodists, Samuel Austin Worcester and Elizur Butler, were arrested and chained.

The Trail of Tears

"... The Chief Justice has made his ruling, now let him enforce it."
— Andrew Jackson

When the case was appealed to the Supreme Court, Chief Justice John Marshall ruled that Indian tribes or Nations had always been considered distinct, independent political communities and retained their original natural rights. In the case of the Cherokee Nation, for whom the appeal had been originally introduced in the 1832 case of Worcester V. Georgia, Justice Marshall said: "The Cherokee Nation...is a distinct community occupying its own territory, with boundaries accurately described, in which the laws of Georgia can have no force, and which the citizens of Georgia have no right to enter, but with the assent of the Cherokees themselves, or in conformity with treaties, and with the acts of Congress."[26] President Jackson is quoted as saying, "The Chief Justice has made his ruling, now let him enforce it."

In 1835, a faction of Cherokees more in sympathy with the United States signed a removal treaty, the Treaty of New Echota. Jackson lobbied the U. S. Senate to ratify the treaty in 1836, where it passed by one vote. This led in 1838, under President Martin Van Buren, to the forcible relocation by the U. S. Army of the Cherokees to Indian Territory (now Oklahoma) in what became known as the Trail of Tears. The removal of the nations commenced and a trail of tears streamed westward. Even today, Native American United Methodists and other religious groups sing hymns that were sung on the Trail of Tears. Some are remembered as being sung in the evening to give strength to their young women who were being assaulted beyond the camp by the soldiers who were escorting the people to the new Indian Territory. "One Drop of Blood" was actually composed on the trail by the Cherokee. Sung today, it still brings tears to the gathered worshipers. "Heaven is Beautiful" is another Cherokee hymn remembered as a song of reassurance. "Prayer to the Holy Spirit," and "Worth of the Soul" are sung today by the Choctaw. According to Billie Nowabbi (Choctaw), and David Adair (Cherokee), nine hymns are remembered today from the Trail of Tears. The rest have been lost to history.

While some missionaries were committed to the rights of Indians in Georgia, Alabama and Mississippi, the Tennessee Methodist Conference was unwilling to support its missionaries in this enterprise. The conference's response was simply to express sympathy with the Indians and affirm its own passion for the conversion and salvation of Native souls. Not only did the conference refuse to support their missionaries in this matter, it rebuked them in a resolution expressing regret for their actions. The Removal Act was implemented by army troops who burned Indian homes and captured men and women to be imprisoned in concentration camps. If the family structure of "civilized" Indians could be destroyed so aggressively by government action, it was only a foretaste of things to come on the so-called American Frontier.

CHAPTER 3

Christian Impact on Native Women and Families

On the American frontier, images and roles of Indian women and families would quickly be threatened as the westward stream of immigrant populations began trickling and then flowing toward the west. Once again, immigrant value systems failed to reconcile what they felt and experienced with what their culture had taught them to see. Stereotypes were fashioned that gave shape to the "squaw" mentality and a view of Native women as little more than slaves doing the bidding of Native men. In their report to the yearly Meetings of Friends of New England and New York in 1843, John Lang and Samuel Taylor described the conditions of the tribes of Indians west of the Mississippi–especially those now living in the new Indian Territory (now Oklahoma) to which Jackson's "removed" Indians had been sent. Women, as they viewed them, were "...generally industrious, performing the greater part of the manual labor both in the camp and on the land. They look dejected and appear more like slaves than otherwise."[27]

We understand what Lang and Taylor saw. What we do not know is what they did not see. Did they know the cultural practices of the people they were observing? Did they understand how children played together or what games they enjoyed and what those games taught them? Did their male eyes and cultural biases pre-determine how they saw and processed their observations? Would a report by two women produce different findings, see different phenomena, understand with a different worldview? I remember a three-day meeting of the Theology in the Americas project in one of our Six Nations camps in the mountains. The non-native women participants watched the Clan Mothers and other women of our Nations preparing the food and doing heavy work in preparation for the meals and the gifts of hospitality. It was obvious that the non-Native women were becoming increasingly uncomfortable as the Native men did nothing to assist the Clan Mothers. Finally, a group of women gathered to question the Clan Mothers as to why the men were not helping. One of the principle Clan Mothers replied that food preparation was a sacred responsibility reserved for women and men were forbidden from touching the food in its preparation. We have no evidence that Lang and Taylor experienced such a lesson by eating with the Six Nations Clan Mothers.

Lang and Taylor divided Native people into three distinct classes. "First, those that are pretty well civilized and appear intelligent. Second, those who may be reckoned among the half civilized or apprentices in civilization. Third, those that have made but little improvement in their dress and manners. They are cultivators of the soil and have generally given up the hunt but are dissipated."[28] Referring to the Choctaw Indians, the report outlined an important feature of a plan about to be adopted by the Choctaw Council that would educate the female children of the nation in a place several miles from the site for education of males. Eighteen thousand dollars was appropriated by the government for this project and it was reported that the Methodists were to have control of the school at Fort Coffee in the Indian Territory.[29]

METHODISTS, MISSIONS AND NATIVE WOMEN

Not surprisingly, it was with the promise of government assistance that Methodists began to establish mission circuits and stations among other Native populations. This support spawned a series of mission efforts among many nations. In addition to the

Choctaw, it included the Wyandot, Shawnee, Creek, Kickapoo, Potawatomi, Chippewa, Flathead, Nez Perce, Cherokee, Kansas and Alaska Natives. Generally these were primary mission attempts. Methodists eventually ministered to large numbers of Indians throughout America by virtue of their rapid growth and the establishment of conventional churches close to Native populations. Primary Methodist mission work was relatively little and late since by 1907, only forty ordained missionaries and one school were to be numbered among their efforts by various journals of the day.[30] Also, by this date, churches ceased receiving funds from the government for educational purposes.

Overlooked or ignored by both church and state was the extraordinary history and role of women in the various Indian nations. Women controlled large numbers of tribal social and political organizations. In such nations as the Iroquois, Sioux, Creek, Choctaw, Chickasaw, Seminole, Navajo and various Pueblos, descent of tribal membership or citizenship in a clan or tribal family was often traced through the female line. Matrilineal characteristics included being heads of clan (or family) organizations, determination of the inheritance of personal and common property and titles of various chieftainships of the nation. In many cases, women exercised the right to elect the male candidates to lead the nation or to raise up chiefs from their own clans (families). Women might also exercise the right to initiate the removal of leaders from office should they fail to attend to the needs of the people. Women owned certain possessions and could dispose of them as they pleased. They also owned the implements of cultural survival as well as directing the use of tribal lands supplying food, shelter and the necessities of life. The home and its furnishings belonged to the woman; the man merely shared in its comforts. In some Native societies, a

Overlooked or ignored by both church and state was the extraordinary history and role of women in the various Indian nations.

woman could expel a man from her household and be supported by the customs of the society. In such communities, women named the children and provided their education. In many Native societies, women held power and assigned authority to the men as together they attended to the political and economic welfare of the nation.

In spite of the church's conclusions and confusions about the role of women in Indian society–whether in a matrilineal or patrilineal society–it was the job of the women to shoulder and to scrupulously exercise social, political and religious authority. Methodist women's societies zealously supported mission programs but failed to perceive the true nature of their sisters' plight. In 1869, the publication of the Methodist Woman's Missionary magazine, *The Heathen Woman's Friend*, would attempt to give guidance to Methodist women in their assistance to and support of Native women. Guided by these sentiments and the commitments of their personal faith, it was Methodist women, many of whom were wives of the circuit-riding ministers, who developed ministries of care among the tribes in whose land they traveled or lived. Even so, Western notions of paternalism and cultural lifestyles would take their toll on Indian civilization. To understand the serious dynamics at work in the deterioration of Indian cultures, one must continually scrutinize the history of church/government relations and their impact on the administration of the Indian "civilizing" process.

To understand the serious dynamics at work in the deterioration of Indian cultures, one must continually scrutinize the history of church/government relations and their impact on the administration of the Indian "civilizing" process.

While Indian women were always the unseen moorings of Native family life and culture, it is important to note that in the late 1970's, Indian women came together in Rapid City, South Dakota, to form WARN (Women of All Red Nations). The formation of WARN was a public announcement that Indian women were not going to allow the continued marginalization of

Indian communities, families and children. They declared that they would work together and with other entities to preserve Indian communities, sovereignty, self-determination and the sanctity of Indian life. WARN eventually became absorbed into other Indian organizations as Indian Country developed new strategies to fight for survival.

Understandably, most earlier mission work was conducted among European immigrants as circuit riding preachers pushed west with waves of land-hungry people eager to fulfill the promises of Manifest Destiny. Like other major denominations, the Methodists played a major role in opening the land to white settlement and shared with other denominations a peculiar complicity in aiding government objectives toward the subjugation of Indian nations. The frontier preacher Peter Cartwright summed up the widespread fear of Indian societies when he called them the "bloody and hostile savages."

The itinerancy and the short tenure of ministers appointed to their posts contributed to the weakness of Methodist Indian mission work. Again, the most substantial work was accomplished among Native people when districts and conferences were formed and churches were built to serve the more permanent population of immigrants. Mission work was also disrupted by the ongoing uprooting of Indian populations and their removal to reservation areas, a common occurrence during the mid-nineteenth century.

Historical themes of the education and domestication of Indians continued to dominate the "civilizing" process and led to competition among the denominations for government funds and authority. In this sense Christianity, even indirectly, became an instrument of the state. Clergy and missionaries were used in obtaining land cessions and negotiating treaties. United States Army officers in league with church agencies established and maintained many mission stations and schools throughout Indian country.

Remarkably reflective of this process was the missionary work of Jason Lee in Oregon. Having been sent by the Methodist Mission agency in New York to the Oregon Territory in 1833, Jason Lee established a mission to Indians that evolved into playing a key role in establishing a provisional government on behalf of the United States. While he schooled Indian children, his lasting imprint was the creation of a school for immigrant children that became Willamette University. Today, Jason Lee's statue stands in Statuary Hall in the United States Capitol in Washington, DC, one of two statues representing the state of Oregon.

The issue of the separation of church and state, although seriously raised during the period of eastern removal, did not become a major question for the churches until later in the twentieth century. There were times when this philosophy could be set aside, as witnessed by a resolution passed by a Methodist annual conference in 1907 stating that it was not expedient for any member of the conference to hold any office of profit or honor in the government of the United States, except in the case of missions to Indian tribes. Surely this was a carryover from an earlier day when a superintendent was appointed by the bishop to oversee the concerns of the Indian Mission Conference to "... attend to all the interests of our missions and schools...as those interests may be connected with the government of the United States, and with the Indian school fund. He may visit Washington City once a year or oftener..."[31] Alas, twentieth century America continued to live on the promise of its earliest dreams and the church continued to play a significant role in the subjugation of Native nations.

THE FINAL STAGES OF INDIAN TREATIES

The United States continued to sign treaties with Indians until 1871 when the treaty system was abolished. Indians were not, however, treated as citizens of separate sovereignties. During the 1850s and 1860s, the treaty process became a device for weakening the independence of tribal governments. It promoted the further encroachment of Congress and government agencies on the day-to-day management of tribal societies. New land laws, more immigrants from abroad and the construction of roads and railways westward resulted in demands to reduce Indian land holdings and clear tribes out of the way of Western settlement. The army continued to fight Indians and manage their affairs after the Civil War as officers returned to their vocations as Indian fighters and agents.

Treaty of Fort Laramie

Few tribes in the nineteenth century would follow the Cherokees and the other southeastern tribes in accommodating government practices of removal. The Western tribes were keenly aware of the government's intentions to rob them of their valuable resources, displace them from their homes, attack and subvert their chosen leaders, defile their religious and ceremonial life and interfere with family relations, dress, and language. The 1868 Treaty of Fort Laramie in the Dakota Territory, signed on behalf of the United States by General William T. Sherman and other "Indian Commissioners," was one of the last great treaties to be entered into by a powerful Indian Nation. This instrument was intended to cease forever the hostilities between the several bands of Lakota (Sioux), the Arapaho and the United States, while expressing a desire for peace and a pledge to honor it. Anyone violating this agreement would be delivered to the United States for trial and punishment according to the laws of the government. It gave ownership of the Black Hills (now in South Dakota) to the Lakota, as well as hunting rights in South Dakota, Wyoming and Montana. The Powder River Country would be closed to all whites. The Paha Sapa (Black Hills) are today, and have been from time immemorial, the primary sacred place for the Seven Band Lakota and other Indian Nations. In a sense, this region is the Native equivalent of Christian seminaries. It is the place where Native young people go seeking vision quests and learning of their place in the universe under the guidance of one of the spiritual leaders of the people.

The seventeen articles of the treaty included financial incentives for the Indians to become farmers and stipulated that minors would receive English educations in mission buildings. The treaty further stipulated that white teachers, blacksmiths, a farmer, a miller, a carpenter, an engineer and a government agent would take up residence on the new reservation. The Indians were to allow peaceful transport of settlers through the reservation land and not attack them or scalp white men in the process. Further, the tribal people would allow the construction of roads and railroads and the establishment of military posts around their territory while established access routes that had been used for decades by the settlers would be shut down. Additionally, no white person or persons could settle on reservation lands without the consent of the tribe. To encourage farming, the treaty promised to deliver to each family or lodge one American cow and a pair of "well-broken" oxen.

Article Eleven gave permission for the Lakota to hunt in territories where the buffalo may range "in such numbers to justify the chase." While most treaties did not contain the rhetoric of "...as long as the grass grows, the water flows, the sun shines and the buffalo roam" that we have learned from John Wayne movies, this treaty did highlight the importance of the buffalo in the lives of the Lakota.

It is a matter of some importance that we note this passage in the treaty. Buffalo (Bison) were a way of life for the Plains Indians. In the case of the plains tribes, what the government and Christian missionaries failed to achieve in their attempts to subjugate Indian people, the slaughter of the buffalo by the millions did accomplish. While the tribes would not be defeated by military might, the killing of their leaders or the disruption of their societies, it was the killing of the buffalo that changed the lives of these people. Failing in attempts on almost every level to vanquish the plains people, the one thing left was the destruction of their religion. The elimination of the buffalo had the lasting effect desired by the new government of the United States. Buffalo, after all, were a major source of protein–a major food staple. The skins of the buffalo provided clothing and shelter and their bones were carefully crafted into fine tools. The buffalo also played a major role in Plains Indian religions. The dried skull was colorfully painted and used on the altar of the Sundance ceremonies. It was the White Buffalo Calf Woman who appeared generations ago to deliver a code of behavior in the "Seven Sacred Rituals." She introduced the use of the "sacred pipe" and its spiritual meanings. The United States military called it the "peace pipe" (as would generations of Hollywood Westerns) because it was used to seal treaty agreements and sacred commitments. Today, the sacred pipe can still be seen on the religious altar of the Lakota and other plains peoples. It is used every day by traditional people in the ceremonies of their spiritual leaders. In some cases, it is used today in courts of law instead of a Bible upon which traditional Native people make

In the case of the plains tribes, what the government and Christian missionaries failed to achieve in their attempts to subjugate Indian people, the slaughter of the buffalo by the millions did accomplish.

their oath. The sacred prayer pipe and its ceremonies brought by White Buffalo Calf Woman would keep strong the memory of a unique people. It would propel them through harrowing times of struggle to survive today where both the buffalo and the plains Indians are strongly increasing in numbers

Battle of Little Big Horn /Battle of Greasy Grass

A footnote to history, briefly noted here, reminds us that it was George Armstrong Custer who in 1874 first broke the Fort Laramie Treaty. He led prospectors and speculators into Lakota Country to the Sacred Black Hills (Paha Sapa) where gold was discovered, signaling the beginning of an onslaught of settlers with gold rush fever matched only by the California gold rush in the 1840s. A year later in 1875, Custer swore on the pipe of White Buffalo Calf Woman that he would not fight Indians again. One year later, on June 25, 1876, a few days before the Centennial celebrations of the birth of the United States, Custer was killed along with most of the Seventh U.S. Cavalry in the Battle of Little Big Horn—or the Battle of Greasy Grass, as the Indians would call it. He was attacking the Lakota, Northern Cheyenne and Arapaho because they were wandering from their treaty reservations. It wasn't until one hundred years later, on June 25, 1976, that Native people were allowed to memorialize their Indian dead on the Little Big Horn Battle Field in Montana. Even then, the citizens of the surrounding Montana towns trumpeted alarm and incited the residents to arm themselves and stand guard because they believed the Indians were coming to rob, rape and pillage. During the ceremonies, the Federal Marshals spread out, forming a circle of protection around the various tribal representatives performing the ceremonies. Large numbers of European Custer enthusiasts were advancing toward the center of the battlefield on horses dressed in Custer-like buckskins to commemorate the one hundredth anniversary. The ceremonies ended peacefully and marked the beginning of loosening legal restrictions on tribal religious practices.

PRESIDENT GRANT'S PEACE COMMISSION

The advent of President Grant's Peace Policy and the establishment of a Board of Indian Commissioners (BIC) consisting of denominational representatives generally continued the existing policies involved in Indian mission work. It was this policy, however, that finally uncovered the true nature of how church/government relations had been practiced for many years. On April 10, 1869, Congress authorized the establishment of a ten-member board empowered to exercise "joint control" with the Interior Secretary over departmental administration of Indian appropriations, contracts, personnel, tribal funds and treaty provisions.

Grant used the BIC to shield himself against strong military demands for appointments in the Indian Service and for maintaining full military control over Native populations. The BIC was also Grant's device for sharing responsibility among America's Christian churches for "civilizing" the Native people while dividing the Indian populations and territories among various Christian denominations. Some denominations were later to contend that, except for the Episcopalians, none were allotted their proportionate number of Indians because allocations were not made relative to denominational size. One can only imagine the church lobby in Washington as they sought funds and their quota of Indians to missionize–all in the hope of solving the "Indian Problem." Thus yoked to the government, churches pursued the American dream of assimilating Indians and of transforming them into independent, literate, land-owning farm families.

The first BIC appointees included three Presbyterians, two Episcopalians, two Methodists and one each from the Baptist, Quaker and Congregationalist denominations. All were reportedly wealthy men with a wide range of businesses and occupations. The BIC had originally been proposed by influential church members as an alternative to the Indian Department, established in 1824, and as a solution for struggles for control. The authority exercised by the BIC was minimal–less than that contemplated by the churches, certainly—and in 1874, the members resigned en masse, protesting their lack of power and the non-cooperation of the Interior Department.

> *Thus yoked to the government, churches pursued the American dream of assimilating Indians and of transforming them into independent, literate, land-owning farm families.*

Grant's so-called Peace Policy, while placing the administration of Indian country into the hands of the church, promoted the general practice of moving Native communities to reservations where they could become Christians and agriculturists to prepare them for assimilation into American society. The churches were called upon to guide Indians from savagery to American citizenship by being placed in charge of government schools and exercising power over the appointment of agency personnel and the regulation of funds. Moral justification for the denial of Indian nationhood then, as before, continued to be the greatest factor in the assimilationist policies and practices of the United States toward Indians. This interplay of politics and religion effectively promoted the denial of Indian sovereignty that was the key formula for shattering Indian culture and family systems.

During the life of the BIC in Grant's administration, the Methodists were assigned fourteen Indian agencies to administer–most of them in the northwest. These were difficult days of unrest with the repeated removal of tribes and the failures of the government to fulfill treaty obligations. The church was scurrying to deal primarily with the more settled populations in annual conferences. As a result, the Methodists had established only one mission out of the fourteen agencies assigned them.

THE END OF TREATIES

In a rider to the appropriation bill of 1871, the House of Representatives obtained Senate concurrence to abolish the treaty system. The House of Representatives declared that the President and the Senate could no longer bind the House to the appropriations of money for Indians. Representative Aaron A. Sargent of California declared that "we pay tribute to these Indians not to make war upon us, not to murder our citizens... yet they are simply the wards of the government, to whom we furnish the means of existence, and not independent nations with whom we are to treat as our equals...Has not the comedy of 'treaties,' 'potentates,' 'nations,' been played long enough?"[32]

"Has not the comedy of 'treaties,' 'potentates,' 'nations,' been played long enough?" — Representative Aaron A. Sargent

In the Senate, William Stewart of Nevada supported these sentiments, saying, "I regard all of these Indian treaties as a sham...you can break up this aristocracy, break up these swindling treaties, and let these Indians have their present annuities on the proceeds of these lands...The idea of thirty or forty thousand men owning in common what will furnish homes for five or ten millions of American citizens, cannot be tolerated."[33]

Opponents of the abolition of the treaty system expressed strong warnings that this would be the first step in the final destruction of tribes in which their land would be plundered. The measure was adopted by the Congress without repudiating the treaties that were then still valid although they continued to be eroded by government policy and practice. Future legal relationships would be conducted through the legislative process and through the executive order of the President. A key result would be the shifting of legal claims and appeals to the Federal Courts of the United States.

INDIAN SCHOOLING

Indian schooling became a significant feature of official United States Indian policy in the 1870's. In 1879, a school was created that would influence Indian education to this very day. Modeled after Indian missions schools established by churches, the government opened its first non-reservation school at Carlisle, Pennsylvania.

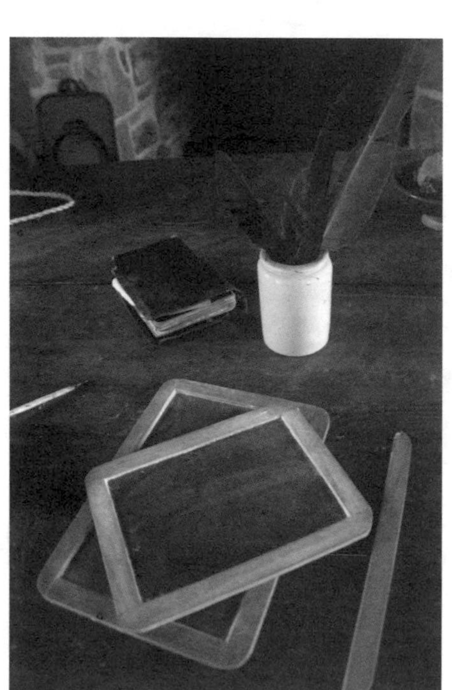

Captain R. H. Pratt became the first superintendent of the Carlisle Indian Training School after serving as keeper of Indian prisoners of war in a federal prison camp in St. Augustine, Florida, where the famous Geronimo had been imprisoned. Older Indians, Pratt argued, were beyond salvation. But the young, separated from the influence of home and tribe, forced to give up their native tongue and culture, immersed in the habits and beliefs of white Americans and taught useful trades and skills, could become functioning, self-reliant adults like other Americans. Pupils were prevented from returning to reservations and urged to remain in the east. They were required to stop speaking their own language and praying their own prayers. They were forced to wear Western styled clothing, eat Western food and observe Christian practices.

The psychological casualties of Indian boarding schools turned Indian communities against the federal schooling of their children. After all, for years they had provided their own academic training based on home rule and now they were thwarted by the imposition of the vast bureaucracy of the federal government. In hindsight, modern scholars would note that with the advent of institutionalized Indian education, Indian children contracted dietary diseases and learned to despise their ancestors, their culture, their religions and their traditional values. The Carlisle School was the culmination of joint government/church cooperation at a time when the government discontinued funding church schools.

As these government schools proliferated across the United States, Indian children were taken from their parents by force and harshly disciplined to remove their Indianness. Interference in parent-child relationships undermined Indian family life and the traditional cultural values that were the very constructs of their existence. One of the more famous graduates of the Carlisle School is Jim Thorpe, the great football player. Today, Thorpe's son and daughters continue to work tirelessly to right the wrongs perpetrated against Native people. In the 1970s, Congress would hear testimony of the work of American drug companies who used Indian school children to test new drugs before marketing them. Pax Riddle's book, *Ruby Loonfoot*, is a fictionalized account of Indian schools and provides a startling window through which to see the impact of these schools on the lives of Indian children. Today, you can still hear the devastating stories told by the Indian elders who were held captive in these schools.

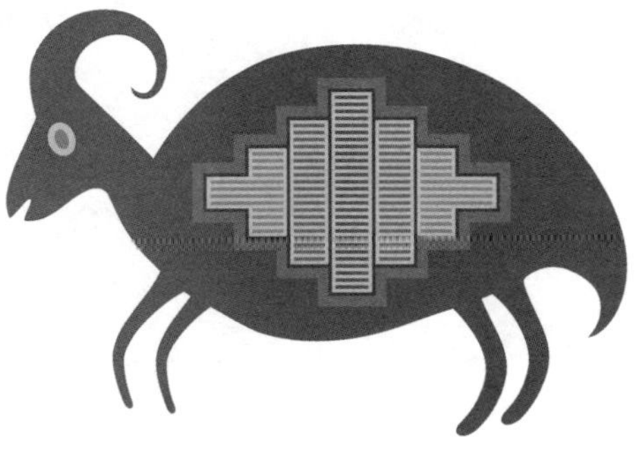

CHAPTER 4

The Great American Takeaway

After the Civil War, settlement of the west brought a sea of immigrants who built towns and villages and expanded established fur trading posts and river towns into booming cities. With them went the web of Western civilization, spun by roads, railroads and telegraph lines. The vast lands occupied by Indians as contrasted with the needs and greeds of the Western-moving population produced a growing consensus that Indians, with their smaller numbers, had far too much land reserved to their own use.

THE DAWES ACT

Those pressures culminated in the Dawes Act, popularly known as the General Allotment Act of 1887, which significantly reduced Indian land holdings. Certainly this action was foreshadowed from the beginning of the European immigration process and in treaties such as the Fort Laramie Treaty of 1869 when the Lakota were to be allotted certain plots for families or lodges to raise crops and cattle. Even treaties of the 1850s and others in the 1860s with tribes of the eastern plains, Minnesota and the Northwest provided for the allotment of land at the discretion of the President.

The model for the impending Dawes Act was the Omaha Treaty of 1854, enabling the President, at his discretion, to have all or part of the Omaha territory surveyed and allotted in quantities of from 80 to 640 acres. It is important to remember that Indians who received allotments were expected to become citizens of the states where they lived. This idea was embodied in agreements as early as the Choctaw Treaty of Dancing Rabbit Creek in 1830. This notion was expanded in the twentieth century as Indians were granted United States citizenship.

The 1887 Dawes Act, or the General Allotment Act, was named after its major sponsor, Senator Henry Dawes of Massachusetts. Even religious and civil bodies and Indian welfare organizations interested in Indian rights supported the measure as providing a means of obtaining for Indians the protection long denied them. Other supporters, though less vocal, were railroad, mining and commercial interests.

President Grover Cleveland signed the bill into law. The act authorized the president to allot 160 acres of tribal land to each head of the family, 80 acres to single persons over eighteen and to orphans, and 40 acres to each remaining person under eighteen. Title to the land was to be held in trust by the government for twenty-five years or longer. At the expiration of the trust period, United States citizenship would be conferred on allottees as well as others who separated themselves from the tribe and adhered to the habits of "civilized life." At the close of the allotment period, surplus lands could be sold. Included in this scheme was the awarding of one-acre allotments of Indian lands to churches to continue their work with Native people.

In 1887, Indian tribes collectively owned about 140 million acres of land. The net effect of this act was to allow over 90 million acres of land to pass to non-Indian ownership within forty-five years. So-called "surplus" Indian land was sold off or opened to land rush races with emigrants staking their claims for both survival and profit. Even at this late date, control of Indians through land acquisition was not the only means employed to wrest their culture from them. Indian religions, ceremonies and various cultural activities were outlawed and suppressed. This led to forcing Indians to abide by non-Indian marriage customs, tribal visiting practices and even determined the age of those who could participate in tribal dances.

WOUNDED KNEE

It was at this time that an Indian prophet from Nevada, Wovoka, preached a message of Indian salvation from white America. His prophecy envisioned the return of the buffalo and the land. His followers joined in the new Ghost Dance religion that both infuriated and frightened the government and its agents. The United States and its military forces realized that it could not suppress the religious pursuits of the Indians as a people and proceeded to arrest and, in some cases, provoke the deaths of Indian leaders.

The advent of the Ghost Dance religion would lead to one of the most senseless tragedies in the history of Indian-white relations. Resorting to military intervention, the United States government engaged in a series of events that led to the tragic massacre of Indian men, women and children at Wounded Knee, South Dakota, in December 1890. Congress later awarded Congressional Medals of Honor to twenty-two soldiers who took part in the massacre. Today, Native people are campaigning to have these medals taken back by Congress.

Charles Eastman, Sioux (Lakota) Indian resident physician of the Pine Ridge Agency, was prevented from going to the massacre site for several days. When he was able to do so, he was confronted with the sight of frozen, grotesque bodies. While he gave medical aid to the survivors, mostly babies protected from gunfire by their mothers' bodies, United States troops dug a large trench and dumped the frozen bodies into a mass grave. Through all of this, there is little evidence indicating that the church raised a voice loud enough to shout down the oppressive forces exterminating a race of people. In twentieth century terms, racism had become a way of life.

By the end of the nineteenth century, Indian communities

and family structures lay in ruin. Indian leadership was dead, imprisoned or apathetic. But even though traditional cultural practices had been disrupted, tradition and language continued to be quietly passed to the young by faithful women away from the gaze of the Indian agents and missionaries There was a cultural flame smoldering that would burn ever brighter as the United States and its churches became preoccupied with other wars and worldly concerns.

TWENTIETH CENTURY REFORMS

"...The problems of urban and industrial life absorbed the attention of the Nation and the only time most Americans thought about Indians at all was when they appeared in the wild west show or as in the case of Jim Thorpe, emerged as an Olympic champion."
— Mary Young

By the end of World War I in 1918, the American people were largely oblivious of the Indian policies carried out in previous years. The average citizen thought the "Indian problem" had been settled with land allotments, schools, missions and treaties. Based on United States census figures of the time, three-fourths of the Indian population had disappeared and some tribes had vanished entirely. As professor Mary Young has pointed out, "...The problems of urban and industrial life absorbed the attention of the Nation and the only time most Americans thought about Indians at all was when they appeared in the wild west show or as in the case of Jim Thorpe, emerged as an Olympic champion."

INDIAN CITIZENSHIP

Approved by Congress on June 2, 1924, the Indian Citizenship Act bestowed U.S. citizenship upon the remaining Native population born within the United States as well granting them citizenship of the state within which they lived. The law, enacted by the U.S. Senate and House of Representatives, resolved:

> "...That all non citizen Indians born within the territorial limits of the United States be, and they are hereby, declared to be citizens of the United States: Provided that the granting of

such citizenship shall not in any manner impair or otherwise affect the right of any Indian to tribal or other property."[34]

The fact is that Indians had been granted citizenship since the early 1800s through treaties as well as through the General Allotment Act of 1887. This act was simply to make explicit what had perhaps been only implicit in some of the earlier agreements. Indians not living on Federal reservations would become subject to state laws. While there were strong sentiments in Congress that Indians should be awarded United States citizenship because of their courageous service in World War I, it is perhaps closer to the truth that this act would, at last, bring all Indian citizens under the authority and laws of the federal government and the states. Women's suffrage efforts resulting in the right to vote and the Nineteenth Amendment to the Constitution in 1920 flag a curious juxtaposition of two contradictory streams of American justice.

...relationships between the United States and Indians... have included peacemaking, diplomacy, armed conflict, tribal removal, subjugation, extermination, concentration, assimilation, termination and self-determination.

INDIAN REORGANIZATION ACT OF 1934

Over a long period of time large numbers of policies and confusing programs of implementation have been adopted by the United States with little apparent thought as to their effect on one another. While there are endless definitions and policies outlining the relationships between the United States and Indian tribes and organizations, they had never been administered in any clear or consistent manner. The foundation for relationships between the United States and Indians comes from the Constitution and has been interpreted through treaties, laws, court decisions and administrative decisions. These relationships have included peacemaking, diplomacy, armed conflict, tribal removal, subjugation, extermination, concentration, assimilation, termination and self-determination. Ultimately, the consequences of these policies have brought about the failure of federal programs and money to eliminate obstacles to self-sufficiency and self-determination for Native people.

Finally, in 1928, Lewis Meriam produced a report called "The Problem of Indian Administration" that led eventually to the Indian Reorganization Act (IRA).[35] In the report, the United States was subjected to close scrutiny in its administration of Indian affairs. Of the General Allotment Law, for example, the Meriam report observed:

"It almost seems as if the government assumed that some magic in individual ownership of property would in itself prove an educational civilizing factor, but unfortunately this policy has for the most part operated in the opposite direction. Individual ownership has in many instances permitted Indians to sell their allotment and live for a time on the unearned income resulting from the sale."[36]

The IRA would become known as the Marshall Plan for American Indians.

While the Meriam report was not a revolutionary document, it did bring together years of observations, neglected recommendations and annual reports, presenting them in a unified and competent study that would shape the decision-making processes of the United States Congress for years to come. Even by the 1970s, not all of the recommendations had been addressed. The Meriam report did place on the front burner the poverty of Indian people: desperately poor health conditions, high infant mortality rates, the prevalence of tuberculosis and trachoma, appalling housing conditions, lack of sanitary provisions, the inadequacy of public health systems and the lack of educational policies. It documented the desperate conditions of Indian children in reservation schools who were being fed on an average of 11 cents a day per child while being forced to do heavy domestic work as a ruse for learning useful industrial skills.

The Meriam survey provided the foundation for the Indian Reorganization Act and its subsequent revisions or amendments. The IRA would become known as the Marshall Plan for American Indians. It set in motion measures that would make Indians self-governing, functioning under their own constitutions and bylaws that would give them authority to "employ legal counsel, prevent sale or encumbrance of tribal land or other assets without the consent of the tribe, negotiate with Federal, State and local governments, determine tribal membership, assign tribal land to individuals...appropriate money for salaries ...levy taxes, license fees...control conduct of members of the reservation by enactment of ordinances, employment of police, establish courts, regulate the conduct of trade, regulate domestic relations and enact other ordinances for the general welfare."[37] They were also to act in a parliamentary fashion and were permitted to enter into contracts and legal agreements for the first time.

Not all tribes voluntarily moved under the new IRA plan. Some chose to go forward with their ancient and never extinguished types of local democracy rather than adopt the parliamentary style of self-government. In the case of nations such as the Six Nations Iroquois (Haudenosaunee), this plan would never be adopted among the traditional elders nor would the granting of citizenship be accepted. As with many other tribes, they were a practicing democracy, an independent sovereign entity, citizens of their own nation. In cases where tribes accepted the IRA plan, divisiveness occurred between the traditional elders who wanted no other government plan and other tribal members who, nonetheless, accepted the IRA and began structuring their IRA tribal governments.

Almost accidental, but key to the historical progress and implementation of the IRA, was the appointment of John Collier as Commissioner of Indian Affairs by President Franklin Roosevelt in 1933. He had been executive secretary of the Indian Defense Association for ten years and brought a conscience and a passion to the job that few could. In his long tenure, Collier would effectively reverse the policy embedded in the General Allotment Act of 1887 and attempt to blunt its anti-Indian impact. He also focused on economic development and the creation of Indian businesses while directing the implementation of health care and educational programs. Significantly, the institutionalized boarding schools for Indians were cut by one-third. Children were moved to community day schools and thousands of children never schooled before were brought into the classroom.

Collier admired Indian value systems and, as Dr. Lawrence C. Kelly indicated, he believed that the "...the preservation of Indian culture was essential to the survival of Western civilization." As Collier himself would say, the 1934 reforms revolutionized United States Indian policy. While previous goals were to destroy Indian society, the IRA gave new birth to Indian progress spelled out in their own terms albeit under the tutelage of United States bureaucracy.[38]

RELOCATION AND TERMINATION

Upon the death of Franklin Roosevelt in 1945, Harry Truman became President. Throughout his tenure and into the presidency of Dwight D. Eisenhower, mischief was afoot again in Washington. The New Deal experienced in the Franklin Roosevelt administration became the "old deal" under Truman and Eisenhower. A series of laws were introduced that would attempt to reverse the progress made between the government and Indian governments.

This crisis began in 1950 when Dillon S. Myer was made Commissioner of Indian Affairs under Truman. Myer had previously been the Director of the War Relocation Authority; that is, the internment program establishing prison camps where 100,000 Japanese-Americans were restrained behind barbed wire. Some of the Japanese prison camps were located on Indian territories–a little known fact of American history. Indian health services, schooling, land-restoration and the protections guaranteed Indians by law were, by Myer's calculations, discriminative privileges. According to John Collier, Myer believed that "...Indian communities were the foes of Indian individuality; and the guarantees against local, state interferences with Indian life-ways and against local property taxation...were gratuitously extended over-privileges. All these conditions must be annihilated..."[39]

The Myer plan came as a thief in the night to create disarray in the daily lives of Indians and their communities.

Although Myer was removed from office by President Eisenhower, the machinery had been set in motion in the massive U.S. bureaucracy. The Myer plan came as a thief in the night to create disarray in the daily lives of Indians and their communities. One of the most destructive measures enacted by Congress was the adoption of Public Law 280. This act empowered any state to "...impose on any and all tribes its own civil and criminal codes and enforcement machinery and thus to annihilate the tribal codes and tribal authorities of self-protection. Then the present Congress assembled and the Interior Department presented a flood of bills, each aimed at Indian destruction..."[40]

The net effect of this campaign was to eliminate the federal trust from Indian lands and to propel the lands onto local tax rolls, repeal the Indian Reorganization Act, outlaw the one hundred tribal constitutions and two hundred tribal corporations and return to a time when Indians had no legal protections. These efforts resulted in termination of federal-tribal relationships by merging tribal interests with individual states. Rural American Indian were resettled in urban areas thereby emptying reservations and ensuring final assimilation. Field relocation offices were initially opened in Chicago, Los Angeles, Salt Lake City and Denver. The Quakers conducted a study of these policies during 1953-1956 and concluded that "It is the policy of Congress, as rapidly as possible to make the Indians within the United States subject to the same laws and entitled to the same privileges and responsibilities as are applicable to other citizens of the United States, to end their status as wards of the United States, and to grant them all of the rights and prerogatives pertaining to American Citizenship..."[41]

Removal of Indians from rural areas to highly urbanized environments produced enormous stress. Promises of job training, health care and housing were rarely delivered and as a newly arrived minority group, discrimination against Indians was rife. Among the new health problems now faced by Indians, alcoholism became part of the price of assimilation. The sentiments of the Bureau of Indian Affairs in 1956 was expressed this way:

> "It is apparent that some people feel that the interests of the tribal groups should be given priority over the rights and interests of the individual Indian…We believe, on the other hand, in the primacy of the individual Indian and his right to choose his own way of life without pressure or coercion... But we are not seeking a solution by trying to break up Indian communities."[42]

President John F. Kennedy and succeeding presidents would continue to grapple with the federal administration of the cultural and civil rights of a unique people. Every political party included in its platforms accommodations for Indian interests. Every presidential office seeker wanted his picture taken with Indian tribal leaders while making promises about what their administration would do for America's Native people.

CHAPTER 5

Disarray to Hope: The New Face of Survival

The 1960s brought new twists to strategies employed by American Indian traditionalists and recently graduated Indians who emerged from universities and graduate schools to become lawyers, physicians and tribal leaders. The increasing Native population captured the attention of political office seekers who saw a new constituency in the body politic. In spite of a tragic and relentlessly violent history among Native peoples and nations, Americans were generally oblivious of Indian policies carried out in previous years. The average citizen thought the "Indian problem" had been settled.

Meetings, protests, oratory and conferences ... were bound together by a common goal to preserve the future of Indian societies against the continuing threat of history and the repeated practices of the United States Government.

New and old Indian leaders knew otherwise. Fueled by the Eisenhower administration's effort to terminate Indian tribes, Native peoples understood that their lands and their civil rights were still in extreme jeopardy. Growing alarm erupted in unprecedented demonstrations, beginning in the1960s and continuing into the 1970s, resulting in the takeover of Mt. Rushmore in South Dakota and Alcatraz Island in San Francisco Bay, the fishing wars in the Pacific Northwest, the takeover of the Wounded Knee community in South Dakota in February of 1973 and many more. The Washington headquarters of the Bureau of Indian Affairs in 1972 became the target of an occupation in 1972. Worried about a repeat performance, the Bureau of Indian Affairs changed the large sign on Constitution Avenue in Washington, D.C. from "Bureau of Indian Affairs" to "Department of Interior South."

If national response to Native survival issues changed only ever so slightly in this historical panorama, the church's role in the quest for human and civil rights among Indians began to shift significantly in this new journey from disarray to hope. Meetings, protests, oratory and conferences took place on the shores of Puget Sound, on the high plains of the Dakotas and the deserts of the Southwest, in the woodlands of Wisconsin and the farmlands of Oklahoma, on the bayous of the Southeast and along the fresh waters of the Northeastern lakes. All were bound together by a common goal to preserve the future of Indian societies against the continuing threat of history and the repeated practices of the United States Government. The policies of the eradication of Native people had to be stopped. Sovereign expressions of Indian nationhood were compellingly expressed in terms unmistakable to the American people and the United States Congress. Assimilation of Indians, theft of land base and natural resources and the elimination of tribal governments had to end with a new era of self-determination and independence. The heyday of outside forces illegally appropriating Indian land, water, fish and "natural resources" would diminish but would bring about a new effort in the United States by anti-Indian groups to divide and conquer.

Surprisingly, the Supreme Court case brought to bear in *Worcester v. Georgia* (U.S. Sup. Ct. 1832) once again cast its historical shadow on the next legal decisions now extending into the twentieth century. How surprising it is for Americans today to realize that Chief Justice John Marshall and the Methodist missionary Worcester would have an impact on the continuing legal claims of American Indians. Marshall had made it clear in the 1832 decision that Indians had a separate constitutional status with jurisdiction over their affairs including governmental and judicial powers that could not be violated. The tribes were now on the move and set about claiming control over their "resources," economies and community life. It is said that in many tribal languages there is not a word for "resources." The term implies taking from the earth. The Indian experience is generally expressed with an understanding that relationships with nature, with the earth, are reciprocal. One cannot take from the earth unless one gives back.

1968 CIVIL RIGHTS ACT

During the Civil Rights era of the 1960s, high expectations were expressed by African Americans who believed that Indians would gladly join the effort to obtain equal rights since they too had been so abused by the events of American history and were in such a desperate condition. While Indian people and organizations supported the Civil Rights movement and worked with leadership to achieve it, few could understand that it was not something they sought for themselves because they were, in fact, sovereign entities bound in a nation-to-nation relationship with the United States. Treaties, we must reiterate, are the law of the land and represent agreements between sovereigns. Natives were not driving toward obtaining a "slice" of America's wealth or fair treatment in the usual context that it was understood during the civil rights struggle. They were working toward the rebuilding of their treaty rights and their recognition as separate, sovereign and unique peoples in the legal web of American jurisprudence.

Missing almost entirely in these challenges to Indian rights was the voice of the churches which was correctly but principally focused on African American rights.

In fact, the 1968 Civil Rights Act brought great losses to Indian nations. Whereas before Native entities had authority over the administration of their own governments, guaranteed by both the Constitution and treaty rights, they now were required to live within certain articles of the Constitution as amended, short-circuiting their independence and sovereignty. Title II of the Civil Rights Act compelled Indian governments to adhere to the first ten amendments of the Constitution, modified to fit the tribal circumstances, thereby taking away from these governments rights and responsibilities obtained through the sacred legal agreements they originally had with the United States. Ultimately, it was the denial of the sovereign immunity of the tribes that weakened their ability to govern fairly. Missing almost entirely in these challenges to Indian rights was the voice of the churches which were correctly but principally focused on African American rights.

LEGAL AND ETHNIC SKIRMISHES

Lip service was in ready supply as Americans generally supported Native people in their bid to remain Indian. Hippie (and later, New Age followers) trivialized native cultural practices and artifacts by creating their own Sun Dances (a traditional sacred ceremony of the plains nations) while crafting dream catchers for their windows or arraying themselves in turquoise as spiritual amulets. Little notice was given to homeless Indians in Minneapolis or Navajo citizens infected by uranium tailings in the streams and rivers of Arizona.

During the 1970s and into the 1990s, various presidents brought varying messages that would sharpen the debate and influence legislation for Indian survival. United States citizens, lulled by their own apathy toward America's first people or simply ignorant of their history or current condition, would awaken soon to the television news reports and newspaper headlines of Indian militancy and actions staged to gain the attention of the world. People were finally moved when they understood that their own agendas were being threatened. "Federal administrators opposed tribes who sought to take over federal programs. State administrators opposed tribal tax

prerogatives. State judges opposed tribal judicial authority. Hunters, fishers and water users opposed tribal hunting, fish-ing and water rights. Environmentalists opposed tribal economic development. Churches and fraternal organizations opposed tribal bingo (at that time). Social workers opposed the Indian Child Welfare Act".[43] National media coverage called attention to half-forgotten issues as Indians entered court to press their claims.

Astonished state legislatures, Bureau of Indian Affairs personnel, Justice Department officials, ranchers and townspeople responded with alarm, fear and anger. The Passamaquoddy and Penobscot Tribes of Maine were demanding the legal return of 60 percent of the state, which they claimed was sold illegally to non-Indians. The case was built not only on the strength of the original treaties with the United States but also with the help of the Indian Non Intercourse Act. In 1790, George Washington had told the Senecas that this Act was the Indians' guarantee against deceit and fraud and would ensure fair play by the government. Similarly, the Wampanoag Indians' claim to 13,000 acres of the town of Mashpee on Cape Cod, Massachusetts, was strengthened when a U.S. District Court judge rejected a motion from the town to dismiss the Indian claim. Many other Indian nations followed suit. Landmark decisions were handed down into the next decade around Northwest fishing rights, Pyramid Lake Paiute Tribe water use and control, Oneida land claims, services to non-reservation Indians, Indian preference in hiring, issues of state jurisdiction over Indian affairs, state taxation on Indian reservations, tribal powers, Menominee resource rights, Indian religious freedom and the Alaska Native Claims Settlement Act.

Americans continued to awaken to reports in their morning

newspapers on some of the most monumental conflicts between Native Americans and the commercial interests of the United States, conflicts that would become the template of future law and practice. For example, on the Klamath River in Northern California, sports fishing interests were opposing Indians who were waging a battle for the survival of the fish people. The true adversaries in the struggle were those who constructed hydroelectric dams, loggers, and commercial fishing interests.

"Shoot an Indian and Save a deer." "Spear a Squaw and Save a fish."

While Judge Boldt's decision on fishing rights in Washington State was upheld by the Supreme Court, there were renewed attacks on Indian fishing. The Indians of the Skagit River region faced still another adversary as they contended with Puget Sound Power and Light over the licensing and construction of twin nuclear plants one mile from traditional salmon fishing grounds. In Arizona, the Navajo and Hopi faced the destruction of a sacred mountain for the sake of uranium. At Church Rock, New Mexico, nuclear waste spills from the United Nuclear Company were contaminating Navajo water, food and cattle as well as the people themselves. Major corporations continued their attempt to remove mineral wealth–including uranium–from the Black Hills of South Dakota belonging to the Lakota (Sioux) who regarded their mountain as a sacred place and key to their spirituality–theirs through the Fort Laramie Treaty of 1868. The Natives of Michigan and Wisconsin faced resistance to their fishing and hunting rights. Bumper stickers cropped up with slogans such as, "Shoot an Indian and Save a Deer," and "Spear a Squaw and Save a Fish." The lines had been clearly drawn.

Modern presidents brought new messages that would alter Thomas Jefferson's Indian philosophy. Jefferson had written of the Indian: "The ultimate point of rest and happiness for them is to let our settlements and theirs meet and blend together, to intermix, and become one people…." The new message was that Indians should give white men the land they wanted in exchange for what the Indian lacked, the white people's way of life including customs, education, religion and technology. While John F. Kennedy seemed disposed to treat Indians fairly, he had little time to implement clear policies to express his intentions. In 1968 President Lyndon Johnson declared, "We must affirm the right of the first Americans to remain Indians while exercising their rights as Americans. We must affirm their rights to freedom of choice and self determination." He further proposed new goals for federal-Indian relations in a Special Message on "The Forgotten American" delivered to Congress March 6, 1968: a goal that ended the old debate about "termination" of Indian programs and stressed self-determination; a goal that erased old attitudes of paternalism and promoted a partnership of self-help:

> "Our goal must be: A standard of living for the Indian equal to that of the country as a whole. Freedom of choice–an opportunity to remain in their homelands, if they choose, without surrendering their dignity; an opportunity to move to the towns and cities of America, if they choose, equipped with the skills to live in equality and dignity. Full participation in the life of modern America, with a full share of economic opportunity and social justice. I propose, in short, a policy of maximum choice for the American Indian. A policy expressed in programs of self-help, self-development and self determination."[44]

"Our goal must be: A standard of living for the Indian equal to that of the country as a whole."
– Lyndon B. Johnson

United Methodist Senator George McGovern introduced substitute Congressional legislation that would begin to implement new measures reversing established laws that had prevented Indian self-determination. President Johnson's "War on Poverty" would bring assistance to large numbers of urban and rural Indians while, surprisingly, loosening the stranglehold on tribal autonomy.

It was President Nixon who in 1970 denounced the termination policy of the Eisenhower administration (failing to mention his role at that time as Vice President), honing Johnson's statement to a finer point:

> "This, then must be the goal of any new national policy toward the Indian people: to strengthen the Indian's sense of autonomy without threatening his sense of community.... There is no reason why Indian communities should be deprived of the privilege of self-determination merely because they receive monetary support from the federal Government. Nor should they lose federal money because they reject Federal control."[45]

"The time has come to break decisively with the past and to create conditions for a new era in which the Indian future is determined by Indian acts and Indian decisions."
– Richard Nixon

Thought to hold one of the more enlightened perspectives on Indian affairs, Nixon espoused policies that would ensure the right of Indian people to choose their own destiny and allow Indian leaders to govern their own communities. Nixon further affirmed this position by declaring in a special message to Congress in 1970, that the historic relationship between the Federal Government and Indian communities would not be abridged without Indian consent and made accommodations for Indian control and operation of federally-funded Indian programs. His strongest statement in that message to Congress affirmed that, "The time has come to break decisively with the past and to create conditions for a new era in which the Indian future is determined by Indian acts and Indian decisions."[46]

Nixon's Commissioner of Indian Affairs, Louis Bruce (son of a Mohawk Methodist minister) was to be the instrument for carrying out the president's policies. He accepted the position because of the ostensible integrity of Nixon's Indian policies.

Later in the administration when Nixon was beset with other worries, Bruce fell out of favor with the president because of his relentless advocacy for Native people. Bruce would tell you that his crowning achievement was being fired by President Nixon because Bruce took him seriously and assumed he really intended to deliver on Indian self-determination. At a later time, because of disagreements related to the administration of the Department of Interior (which houses the Bureau of Indian Affairs), Secretary Walter Hickel would also be fired by Nixon.

Over forty years before Nixon, the writers of the Meriam Report suggested:

> "The people of the United States have the opportunity, if they will, to write the closing chapters of the history of the relationship of the national government and the Indians. The early chapters contain little of which the country may be proud. It would be something of a national atonement to the Indians if the closing chapters should disclose the national government supplying the Indians with an Indian Service which would be a model for all governments concerned with the development and advancement of a retarded race."[47]

During the Nixon administration there was a willingness to seriously consider the essence of this report. The stage was set with the right attitudes and its political actors were infused with a willingness to forge a new historical relationship with American Indians employing some of the highest expectations of the Federal Government along with the resolve to engage Indians in finding solutions to their own challenges.

THE AMERICAN INDIAN POLICY REVIEW COMMISSION (AIPRC)

These sentiments evolved into legislation never before enacted in American history, the advent of the American Indian Policy Review Commission (AIPRC). Created by joint Congressional action in January of 1975, this historic commission undertook a two-year project guided by the oversight of three senators, three members of the House of Representatives, and five Indians serving as commissioners. The investigations and final legislative recommendations would be produced by Indians themselves recruited from the various tribes across the nation. The AIPRC would help right the disasters of history's many injustices and had the potential to chart the course of federal-Indian relationships for the next one hundred years. By law, the commission was chartered to study and analyze the Constitution, treaties, statutes, judicial interpretations and executive orders to determine the nature of the unique relationship between the federal government and Indian tribes and the land and resources they controlled. The commission would review the policies, practices and structure of federal agencies charged with protecting Indian resources and providing services to Indians. It also received a special mandate from Congress to conduct an exhaustive management study of the Bureau of Indian Affairs.

Working under the joint appointment of the United States Senate and the House of Representatives for the AIPRC as liaison with Indian tribes, I witnessed the daily unfolding of this extraordinary history. In nearly every commission meeting and in innumerable hearings conducted throughout the United States, the issue of Indian sovereignty was a primary agenda item. It became clear early on that the commission would support sovereignty and Indian self-determination. Tribal governments should have jurisdiction over decisions affecting reservations including land use, natural resources and other economic interests. Congress should exercise its legally derived responsibilities, but tribes would have local decision-making power.

This point, of course, was key to most of the controversy in and out of Indian country. Given the wealth of natural resources, tribes could set about managing their own contracts and development projects without undue interference from the government. Indians controlled perhaps 30 percent of America's future energy and close to 80 percent of its uranium.

This point was not lost on energy-producing tribes. Taking their cue from third world countries, these tribes consolidated control over their natural resources on treaty-protected lands and, in 1975, formed the Council of Energy Resource Tribes (CERT). Some called this coalition the Indian OPEC. Then Navajo Nation Chair Peter MacDonald said of this historic moment, "...a subsector of American society that has been overlooked for hundreds of years, which inhabits less than five percent of the land that was once theirs, today finds itself the owner of a potential energy resource whose wealth is so vast it has not yet been measured." To which we might add, "the meek shall inherit the earth." Whereas before the government would enter into deals with energy corporations leaving Indians with only pennies, the new Indian tribal coalition would bargain with the same corporations and reap vast rewards through their own contracts.

"...a subsector of American society that has been overlooked for hundreds of years, which inhabits less than five percent of the land that was once theirs, today finds itself the owner of a potential energy resource whose wealth is so vast it has not yet been measured."

— Navajo Nation Chair Peter MacDonald

Of the many significant recommendations going to Congress from the AIPRC, none was more dramatic than the call for the dismantling of the Bureau of Indian Affairs and the creation of a separate, independent agency whose head would be a cabinet-level appointment. Of course, this has not yet occurred. Every decision made by tribal governments is still subject to review by the Secretary of the Interior. The more intricate legal recommendations by the commission focused on tribal jurisdiction, age-old questions related to tribal courts and the way the judicial process dealt with Indians and non-Indians on Indian land.

Equally complex were recommendations affecting non-reservation Indians living in cities and rural areas (today, it is estimated that at least 65 percent of Native people in the United States live in urban areas). If those persons were to receive the benefits to which they are legally entitled, what sort of delivery mechanisms could be established off the reservations to assure the extension of social services? A new Senate Select Committee on Indian Affairs would be created to oversee the development of new Indian laws and implement those recommendations provided through the AIPRC. Of the more than two hundred legislative recommendations made by the Indian Policy Review Commission in 1977, 113 were enacted into law.

...sovereignty...is the issue that characterizes American Indians as "untimely survivors".

Representative Lloyd Meeds, Democrat from Washington State and vice-chair of the commission, was the single opposing voice to the conclusions outlined in the AIPRC report to Congress. Political difficulties at home and genuine dissent from the findings of the commission moved him to conclude:

> "...We have missed it because the valid and achievable recommendations of the Commission will be lost in a cloud of controversy over others which are nether legally sustainable nor politically achievable...much of the report is neither legally nor historically accurate. Most of the inaccuracy springs from the initial erroneous conclusions regarding sovereignty, jurisdiction and trust responsibility. These very basic and fundamental errors permeate and taint almost every part of the report."[48]

ANTI-INDIAN BACKLASH

Meeds would find supporters for his objections to the basic questions of Indian sovereignty in nearly half of the states of the union. This is the issue that characterizes American Indians as *untimely survivors*. Certainly, no one seriously considered the possibility of Indian survival into the latter half of the twentieth century. By now, all the land and its natural resources should belong to the majority culture. But this has not happened. And because it didn't, "backlash" organizations coalesced powerful lobbies to resist increased judicial and legislative acknowledgment of Indian rights with local chapters established in some twenty-three states. Their membership included non-Indian ranchers, sports enthusiasts, fishing interests and others.

Groups such as the Interstate Congress for Equal Rights and Responsibilities proclaimed themselves the new defenders of the "civil rights of non-Indian people." They petitioned the United States government to void past treaties and demanded that Indians give up tribal identity to be assimilated for the good of the country. Such backlash organizations –along with survivalists–formed the precursors of today's militia groups.

I can well remember the tense moments in the basement of the United Methodist Church in St. Ignatius, Montana on the border of the Flathead reservation where I mediated a nearly violent confrontation between the founder of the Montanans Opposed to Discrimination (a branch of the Interstate Congress for Equal Rights and Responsibilities) and local Indian representatives. The meeting was arranged in an attempt to reduce the dangerous intensity of conflict and to avoid physical violence between the white and Indian communities. The two sides were wrestling with the controversy of Indian water rights and other equally inflammable issues, producing dangerous hostilities. Tensions continue to mount as through the years American corporations learned they could no longer enter into cozy relationships with governmental agencies to have free access to remaining Indian land with reserves of coal, oil, gas, shale, water, timber and other resources. Also, ranchers and farmers have not accepted happily the decisions of tribal governments to terminate non-Indian land leases in order to allow Indians the opportunity of developing the land themselves.

A significant political cornerstone was laid in 1994 that ushered in the fulfillment of anti-Indian sentiment. The 1994 "Contract With America," initiated in the House of Representatives with Newt Gingrich, would not recognize the treaties and agreements reached between the United States and sovereign tribal entities. In fact, through its ten-point program, the Contract actually moved toward providing the "final solution" for Native Americans and the termination of their right to exist as a unique people through measures that would reduce the federal bureaucracy and have a negative impact on the protection of Indian sovereignty and treaty rights oversight all the while slashing the federal budget and Indian programs.

THE CHURCH RESPONDS

In a statement on "The United Methodist Church and the American Indian (Native Americans)", The United Methodist Church at its 1976 General Conference adopted a resolution calling for:

> "The United Methodist Church especially...its congregations to study and give consideration to the recommendations of the American Indian Policy Review Commission... which...for three years has studied and analyzed treaties, statutes, agreements, and executive orders of the United

States government in order to clearly determine the rights of American Indians and to make recommendations which can develop a new and more just policy through legislation of the United States Congress..."[49]

This new policy, of which the foregoing is but a part, signaled a new day in The United Methodist Church's relationship with American Indians. It also coincided with and perhaps provided impetus for other major denominations to focus on their relationship with America's Native people, spawning a spate of "apologies" to Native people similar to the United Methodist apology adopted in General Conference in 1992 and reaffirmed in 2004. The 1976 United Methodist resolution on Native Americans was supplemented in the General Conference of 1980, with language directing:

> "The United Methodist Church (and especially) its congregations to support the needs and aspirations of America's Native peoples as they struggle for their survival and the maintenance of the integrity of their culture in a world intent upon their assimilation, Westernization and absorption of their lands and the termination of their traditional ways of life. Moreover, we call upon our nation, in recognition of the significant cultural attainments of the Native peoples in ecology, conservation, human relations, and other areas of human endeavor, to receive their cultural gifts as part of the emerging new life and culture of our nation."[50]

A major shift of the corporate church to preoccupations of personal "sins" has blunted the force of its historic ability to address corporate "sins" of significant magnitude.

Implementation of this call by the church has been slowed by the current preoccupations with international conflicts, racial and religious wars, loss of church membership and a general aversion to dealing with corporate church controversies around racial and ethnic issues. A major shift of the corporate church to preoccupations of personal "sins" has blunted the force of its historic ability to address corporate "sins" of significant magnitude.

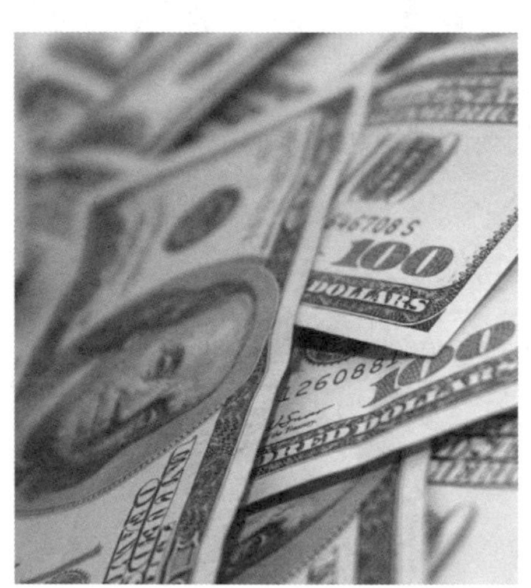

THE REAGAN ERA OF TERMINATION

The churches could not have anticipated the next chapter in Indian history that would unravel some of the best efforts of both the church and the tribal entities themselves. Perhaps no single individual would wield more power to reverse the encouraging trends toward Indian self-determination than President Ronald Reagan would during the 1980s. While campaigning for the presidency, Reagan was asked what lives he had wished to live. He said he was "fascinated by those who saw this new world–Cortes, Lewis and Clark, Father Sierra–when it was virtually untouched by man." At the end of his presidency when asked about the justification for Indian policy, Reagan replied, "Maybe we made a mistake in trying to maintain Indian cultures. Maybe we should not have humored them in wanting to stay in that kind of primitive life-style. Maybe we should have said, 'No, come join us. Be citizens along with the rest of us.'"[51] By the end of 1983, Indian reservations were in a national emergency. Not only were large percentages of social services funds eliminated, Indian aid was cut by more than a third. Reservation unemployment, already 50 to 60 percent, shot to 80 and 90 percent. In the cold winters of the early 1980s, cattle were starving on the plains and Hollywood celebrities were enlisted to raise money to keep both Indians and cattle alive. Reagan regularly vetoed bills that would provide cash settlements due to Indian tribes. Such was the new Era of Termination, an era characterized by neglect and inhuman treatment of America's first people.

CHAPTER 6

An Era of Progress

In 1972 while initiating plans for a reduction on BIA programs, Bureau of Indian Affairs Commissioner Louis R. Bruce, a United Methodist, said:

> "Developing Indian economies does not mean really locating non-Indian industry close to or on the reservations so that these corporations can enjoy a cheap labor supply. It means the development of truly Indian economic systems so that a dollar once earned by an Indian citizen can be spent and kept moving throughout an Indian economy, thus developing that economy and making a maximum impact upon that community…I want to see Indian economies where dollars move from Indian hand to Indian hand and are not drained out by those non-Indians cities that develop and grow and feed upon Indian reservations."

This was not just a statement about self-determination or economic development. It was a sentiment undergirding the needs of people who had the same hopes and aspirations, fears and concerns as the rest of the American people. The decades of the 1970s and 1980s would produce some of the most far-reaching advances for Indians that had been achieved in at least one hundred years and some disappointments as well. Native survival goals would now be spoken of in terms of development goals–not necessarily quantifiable, monetized goals, but a sustained and, it is to be hoped, self-sustaining exercise of control over their own lives.

As the Christian churches shaped their Indian policies, Indian young people seeking spiritual sustenance would return to the Longhouse ceremonies in the Northeast, the Sundance on the plains, the Roundhouse observances in the south and the sweat lodge ceremonies… in record numbers.

Even the National Council of Churches in Christ (NCCC) dusted off its ancient policy statements on Indians in 1978 and attempted to fashion a new policy consistent with their more enlightened positions on women, racism and environmental concerns. As a member of the Governing Board of the NCCC at that time, my Indian colleagues and I found it remarkable that there was so little enthusiasm for a new Indian policy. When we forced the issue in plenary, stonewalling delayed the process until the NCCC introduced another measure recognizing Yasser Arafat's Palestinian Liberation Organization (PLO). With discussions of the rights of Palestinians, there was suddenly a room full of church representatives speaking about sovereign rights, treaty obligations, land base, self-determination and nationhood. These were the very issues we had introduced in the new Indian policy for which there was little interest. Finally, with the recognition of the PLO as the representative body for Palestinians, the just claims of Native Americans were recognized and a common language emerged that, in some cases, harkened back to the member church judicatories. The policy adopted by the NCCC was modest, but it provided the policy base for the significant work in which that ecumenical body engaged over the next two decades.

NATIVE ALASKA'S TIME IN THE SUN

Throughout all of the negotiations around Native societies and treaties and cultural issues, Alaska was nowhere on the horizon until it became a state in 1959. Even then, commercial interests fueled discussions around the statehood act. These interests were already at work making plans for a trans-Alaska pipeline to transport oil deposits from Prudhoe Bay. Alaska Natives, of course, claimed they had always owned the land. The Alaska Native Claims Settlement Act of 1971 was the direct result of this confrontation. In the deal, consummated at the Alaska Methodist University in Anchorage (now known as Alaska Pacific University), Alaska Natives gave up their title to most of the state but retained ownership of about 44 million acres and a fund of $1 billion. As dazzling an achievement as this seemed to be in the twentieth century, the history of the questions of sovereignty would exact its measure in the agreements. The land would be divided into Native corporations. The absence of tribal governments would mean that the corporation shareholders, the Natives themselves, would be able to individually sell their shares and their land by 1991, thereby introducing the fear of losing Native holdings to developers and oil interests. As economic pressures push the Native people to shift more completely from a subsistence economy to a cash economy, the final outcome is still evolving.

Missionary Work

Alaska missionary work had been initiated in 1886 in Unalaska in the Aleutian chain by the Women's Home Missionary Society (WHMS). Eventually, it resulted in the establishment of the Jesse Lee Home in Anchorage, now the Alaska Children's Service. Mission work spread throughout Southeastern Alaska where the WHMS was responsible for recruiting the first Native minister to serve in Alaska. A frustrating passage occurred when the federal government through the Grant Peace Plan assigned to Presbyterians the right to be the only authorized church to missionize Alaska (although the Methodist Church never recognized such agreements). Nevertheless, with the organization of the Alaska Mission in 1904, Methodists continued developing missions and soon spread throughout all of Alaska.

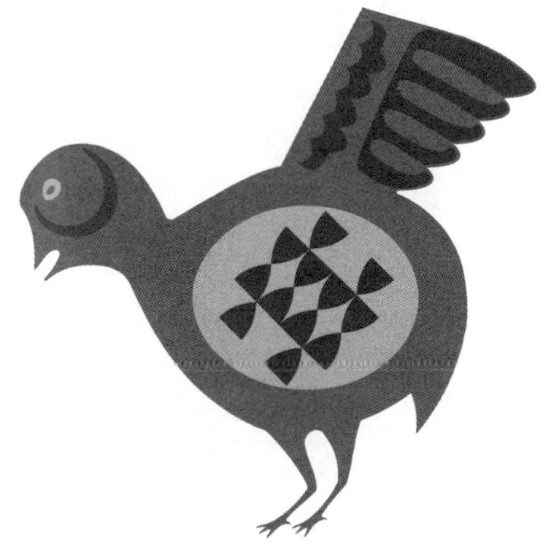

Of remarkable note is the story of Gordon Gould, an Aleut, who as a child was a resident of the Jesse Lee Home. Gordon became an ordained Methodist minister, eventually superintending the Alaska Mission. Over a period of years, administering the mission from his New York office with frequent trips to Alaska, Gordon founded what we now know as Alaska Pacific University. Today, you will find a stained glass window in his honor in the chapel of Garrett-Evangelical Theological Seminary on the campus of Northwestern University in Illinois, memorializing one of the great Methodist leaders of the twentieth century.

THE MENOMINEES FIGHT BACK

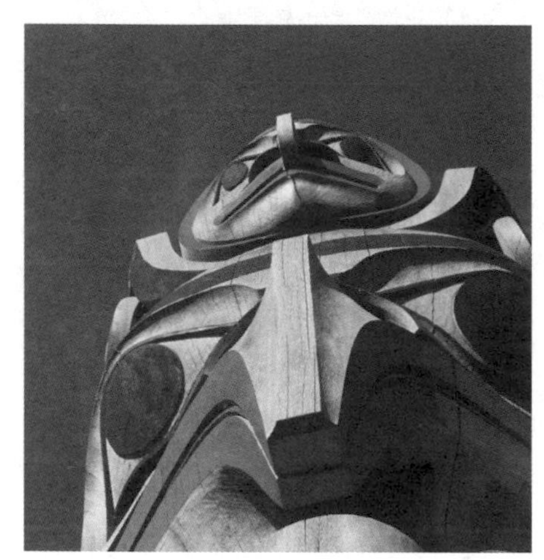

The Menominee Restoration Act of 1973 began the reversal of the termination policies of the previous 100 years. During the Eisenhower administration, the Wisconsin tribe had been terminated because they were thought to be economically self-sufficient, ready to feed themselves, pay taxes and be released from the oversight of the federal government. With that, the vast timberlands held by the Menominee were clear-cut by the United States and the proceeds of the sale were held in the United States Treasury. Led by Ada Deer, a Methodist woman tribal leader, the Menominee fought back in the courts until winning the 1973 decision. Ada later became the fifth Indian to head the Bureau of Indian Affairs for the United States.

INDIAN CHILD WELFARE

A variety of stories contributes to our understanding of this era and the historical transition brought about by these events. While the narratives are plentiful, the use of a few will illustrate the tone and color of this important period. One piece of legislation that would have an impact on churches in general and at least one church specifically was the Indian Child Welfare Act of 1978. I was not a disinterested party in the discussions and formulation of this act. Neither were thousands of Indian families and other Indian adults who were the subject of Indian adoption and the practice of declaring Indian parents incompetent and removing their children from them. Churches had historically played a role in this process but they were perhaps less obvious during the times when Indian boarding schools were founded and children were separated from their families

By 1978, with the scarcity of white children available for adoption and the cost of adopting them into white families, Indian children were highly desirable commodities. At a somewhat earlier time, I had been taken from my Seneca Indian mother and remanded to an orphan's court where, at the age of four, I was adopted by a white family. These practices were common and destructive to Indian family life. The Indian Child Welfare Act was designed to stop the removal of Indian children from their homes. At that time in the 1970s, surveys indicated that between 25-35 percent of all Indian children were separated from their families and either institutionalized, adopted or placed in foster homes. This act would finally recognize tribal jurisdiction over child custody on reservations and would shift many non-reservations cases to tribal courts, in some cases creating cooperative relationships between the tribes and states.

...the American Indian Religious Freedom Act set the course for the legal relief Native people sought to exercise their ancient religious customs.

AMERICAN INDIAN RELIGIOUS FREEDOM

The American Indian Religious Freedom Act of 1978 called for changes necessary for the protection and preservation of the religious cultural rights and practices of the American Indian, Eskimo, Aleut and Native Hawaiians. Although Indians had faced repression and ridicule and had been subjected to coercive Christian conversion efforts, Indian religious freedom was met with less than great enthusiasm by American denominations. Even in the 2000 General Conference of The United Methodist Church, suspicion surrounded the renewal of its own "Native American Comprehensive Plan" and language was adopted directing that the goals of the comprehensive plan would be "Christian." It would seem that Methodism's Indian members were not yet capable of recommending the solutions for strengthening their own Indian churches and recruiting Native persons for ministry. Nevertheless, the American Indian Religious Freedom Act set the course for the legal relief Native people sought to exercise their ancient religious customs.

In *The Soul of the Indian*, Charles Eastman relates: "A missionary once undertook to instruct a group of Indians in the truths of the holy religion. He told them of the creation of the earth in six days, and of the fall of our first parents by eating an apple. The courteous savages listened attentively, and, after thanking him, one related in turn a very ancient tradition concerning the origin of the maize (corn) and how the Great Spirit provided this gift of food. But the missionary plainly showed his disgust and disbelief, indignantly saying: 'What I delivered to you were sacred truths, but this that you tell me is mere fable and falsehood!'" While declaring their own religious traditions to be either infallible or literal truths, non-Indian people had never accorded other religions this privilege.

While the major religions of the world trace their origin back to a specific person or event such as the Exodus, Jesus, Mohammed, or Buddha, for example, Americans failed to see the parallels between their commemorative sacred events expressed in ceremonies and rituals, such as Holy Communion and the Passover, and Native American rituals and ceremonies.

Until the enactment of this landmark decision, the interests of Christianity and those of the federal government were often identical. Dancing of any kind among Indians had been outlawed. Sun Dances of the plains Indians were very threatening to governmental and church progress among tribes. Thirty days' imprisonment was ordered for Native people who participated in traditional rituals and males were required to cut their long hair. Indians using sacred eagle feathers or peyote were often arrested. Sacred lands and sacred places—key to ceremonial observations—were regularly violated with westward expansion. While the major religions of the world trace their origin back to a specific person or event such as the Exodus, Jesus, Mohammed, or Buddha, for example, Americans failed to see the parallels between their commemorative sacred events expressed in ceremonies and rituals, such as Holy Communion and the Passover, and Native American rituals and ceremonies.

It wasn't until the early 1970s that official recognition was afforded to these special places and religious activities. Indian spiritual leaders surfaced to testify about the need to protect Indian religious practices. The Religious Freedom Act fostered a policy to "protect and preserve for American Indians their inherent right of freedom to believe, express, and exercise traditional religions." Paying special attention to the right of access to sacred lands, the first legal action stemming from this act was to legally return the Blue Lake area to Taos Pueblo, followed by the return of Mount Adams to the Yakima Nation. As promising as these developments were, they would be contradicted repeatedly by decisions of the Supreme Court and by Congressional legislative action.

In 1996, President Clinton signed an executive order calling for the protection of Indigenous sacred sites. It was not, however, enforceable. Adding to the headache of sorting out the conflicting interests of these compelling issues, the courts have found that Indian religions are not covered in the First Amendment. In fact, courts have declared that protecting Indian religious freedom is a violation of the First Amendment because it is in violation of the establishment clause to favor Indian religious freedom claims, especially over sacred sites, above other religions. It is important to note that the act assisted traditional Natives in preventing a dam at Kootenai Falls in Montana and the construction of a Forest Service access road near sacred sites in California. It did not, however, halt development in Arizona around Rainbow Bridge and the San Francisco Peaks so often decried by Hopi elders.

Legislative claims, court cases and questions of state authority have followed in quick succession. Cases involving water rights, tribal courts, taxation, fishing and hunting rights, issues of Indian jurisdiction and agricultural and economic development are still the currency used by Native people to ensure their future and the viability of the next generations. The results are still mixed even in a hopeful era. Whilc thc Maine Indian Claims Settlement Act of 1980 involving the Passamaquoddy and the Penobscot resulted in a fund enabling them to purchase 300,000 acres of land and an investment purse of $27 million, the 1985 Supreme Court decision in favor of the Cayuga Nation claim to thousands of acres of land in Central New York had a different ending. This latter decision may well be a bellwether of things to come. History has a long arm and still has its hand on the outcome of critical decisions for Indians. The Cayuga claim relied on the Non Intercourse Act of 1790 and 1807, still in force today, requiring the United States to approve land agreements: "no… conveyance of lands…from any Indian nation or tribe of Indians shall be of any validity…unless the same shall be made by treaty or convention entered into pursuant to the Constitution." The Cayugas had entered into several treaties with the State of New York, but the transactions were never confirmed by the Congress. The claim was denied in 2006 on final appeal.

History has a long arm and still has its hand on the outcome of critical decisions for Indians.

There are few subjects in the history and laws of the United States on which public views are more dramatically and flagrantly erroneous than on the subject of American Indians. This fact has been profoundly accentuated in ongoing attempts by Congress, charged with exercising the "trust responsibility" toward Native peoples, to further erode its responsibilities. Much of this situation stems from the complexity of the vast body of Indian law, based on more than four hundred treaties and statutes and upon thousands of judicial decisions and administrative rulings. It is no wonder that we tire of hearing about the legal findings of one decision or another. But without this knowledge, ignorance will prevail among citizens and parliamentarians.

Native American survival, once thought an ancient and dead issue, is teaching new lessons that speak of contemporary rights and responsibilities that have grown out of a long history of depredation and racial threat. It is generally mistakenly believed that the federal government owes the American Indian the obligation of its trusteeship because of the Indian's poverty or because of the government's wrongdoing in the past. Certainly, American Indians are stricken with poverty, and without question, the government has abused the trust given it by treaty and law. But what is not generally either known or understood even today is that within the federal system, the government's relationship with Indians and their rights holds the highest legal standing and has been tested against current international law.

Native American survival... is teaching new lessons that speak of contemporary rights and responsibilities that have grown out of a long history of depradation and racial threat.

The relationship of American Indians to the United States is a political relationship, a relationship of a weak people to a strong people. It is a relationship of weak governments to a strong government. It is a relationship founded on treaties in which the Indian tribes placed themselves under the protection of the United States and this country assumed the obligation of supplying such protection. Finally, it is a relationship recognized in the laws of the United States as a relationship with domestic, dependent sovereigns.

Through the intervening years, history has brought incalculable damage to Indians, their property and their societies. Tribes have been moved about like livestock until, in some cases, the original homeland was but a legend in the minds of the old men and women. Children had been removed from the family, sometimes by force, and kept in close custody until they lost their original language and all knowledge of who they were, while parents often did not know where the children had been taken or whether they lived. Tribal religious practices, when they were not prohibited outright, were treated as obscenities. Land losses were catastrophic, while the failure of the government to provide economic tools and training for proper land use left the remaining holdings unusable or leased to farmers at starvation rates. The Western style of government penetrated the entirety of Indian life, replacing tribal decision-making practices, demeaning local leadership, weakening the family–and yet was totally oblivious to its inadequacies and its inhumanity.[52]

The recitation of this history is essential in understanding the current threat to Indian rights now being adjudicated through the political process in the United States. Advances made to correct these historical aberrations since 1920 are now being held hostage by Congress and the states in an attempt to bring America back to its "center." This "center" upholds the primary rights of the majority culture but often exempts them from responsibility toward racial and ethnic persons who are subject to alarming social engineering that may deprive them of basic rights which most of them have sought, democratically, to attain.

THE NORTHERN CHEYENNE AND MINING RIGHTS

While the 1970s and 1980s had their moments of victory, they also had their times of angst. Not only were there ongoing conflicts with the United States Government, there were also developing internal conflicts among the Indian nations as well. The Indian Reorganization Act (IRA) of 1934 had provided the almost predictable spectacle of traditional Indians opposing the decisions of the elected (IRA) tribal councils. In Montana, the Northern Cheyenne leased mining and prospecting rights to coal and other resources to companies on over half of their 440,000 acre reservation. As Maria Sanchez, tribal judge, explained it, the tribe became divided over the prospect of strip mining and the disruption of the earth as well as the traditional practices of the people. A group of Northern Cheyennes visited the Pennsylvania and Big Mountain, Arizona, coal fields to examine the historic mining operations there and attempts at reclaiming the land. They returned home to Montana declaring that they would not permit the scarring of the breast of Mother Earth as they had seen it in Pennsylvania and Arizona. The Northern Cheyenne Tribal Council voted unanimously to cancel all existing leases. Internal conflicts ensued with commercial interests, supported by government interests, eventually winning. Today, you can drive through Northern Cheyenne country and see the impact of strip mining on the land as a harbinger of things to come.

WHERE THE PARTRIDGE DRUMS

So tense was the environment in Indian country during this time that the print and television media used plenty of headline ink and broadcast tapes. In August of 1979, the longest siege of Indian country in modern United States history commenced over the confiscation of chain saws by traditional Mohawk Indians resulting from the illegal cutting of trees authorized by elected representatives. Of course, this fracas was not really about trees and chain saws. It was clearly a demonstration of power and authority by the elected (IRA) Mohawk tribal council at Akwesasne (where the partridge drums) in Northern New York over the ancient traditional system of the Hodenosaunee–

the historic confederacy of the Six Nations Iroquois.

State troops were moved in to surround the traditional faction encamped on Racquette Point. Hundreds of armed tribal members threatened to storm the well-armed traditionals to protect what the elected officials called the tax-paying and law-abiding citizens of the reservation and to show support for the state and local police. The state troopers, it turned out, were many of the same actors who had participated in the assault on the Attica Penitentiary with Major Schneeman in command. He was now in command at Akwesasne and, it was reported, saw himself as something of a George Armstrong Custer. The assault never came about as negotiations forestalled what seemed inevitable. The state's motives were always clear. They had been dealing with the traditional Hodenosaunee for over 200 years and were tired of the traditionals opposition to the building of the St. Lawrence Seaway and their claims on land that were still viable instruments of law.

Indictments and arrests ensued as traditional leaders were arraigned and jailed. I played a mediation role in this affair and used United Methodist bail funds from the General Board of Church and Society to bail out those who had been jailed. United Methodists in the surrounding countryside were not pleased. Meeting mornings for breakfast with Schneeman, I learned something of his expectations and what he anticipated in the day ahead. On some occasions he told me that I would not be admitted through the lines to visit the traditional encampment. On those days, I traveled to Cornwall Island in Canada on the other side of the St. Lawrence River where the "Mohawk navy" ferried me across and into the traditional camp. Major Schneeman would later be relieved of his duties and replaced with another commanding officer who had less heroic views of his role and who was better able to moderate the intensity of the confrontation.

During the two-year siege, the traditionals on Racquette Point carried on faithfully in the accustomed manner of the Longhouse. Prayers greeted the new day, press releases were filed, babies were born and people died natural deaths. Finally, by the winter of 1981, hostilities ceased through the intervention of mediation and negotiations through the offices of Governor Hugh Carey. Later, in 1995, while I was traveling with Governor Carey in Ireland, he unburdened himself of his role in this long and difficult conflict. He hadn't spoken of it for years, it seemed, and rehearsing the events with me brought a certain closure to the incident for him.

BLACK MESA

Other ongoing conflicts would be sustained into the new century. In Arizona the Navajo-Hopi Joint Land Use Law was further accentuating conflicts between those two tribal bodies. The law was thought to be necessary because each claimed encroachments by the other on their lands. But nothing was to unite them in common cause quite so decisively as the continued mining of coal that had been going on since the 1960s on Black Mesa, Big Mountain–a sacred place for the Navajo.

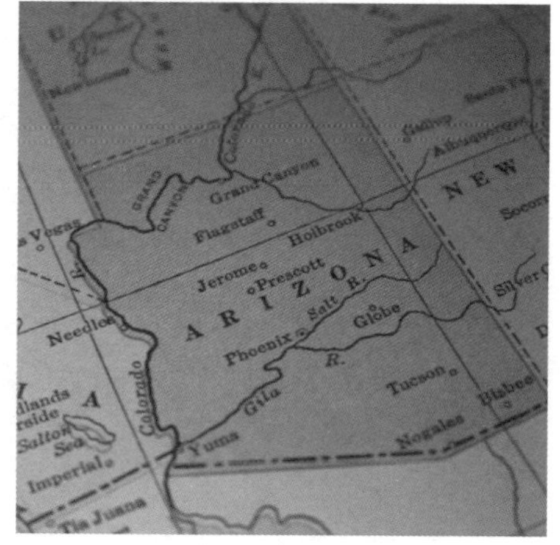

Nothing was to unite [the two tribal bodies] in common cause quite so decisively as the continued mining of coal that had been going on since the 1960s on Black Mesa, Big Mountain–a sacred place for the Navaho.

In the midst of the land use questions and expulsions of Indians from the lands they had used from time immemorial and the confiscation of sheep and cattle by the government, remnants of both Navajo and Hopi held fast to their traditional ways and refused to move. The government's interest in spending millions of dollars providing relocation incentives for the people unabashedly coincided with Peabody Coal's abiding interest in the coal that so richly veined the Black Mesa (hence, its name), supported by both of the elected councils of the Hopi and Navajo. For four decades and in the face of increasing protests from the traditional residents, Black Mesa would become the largest strip mine in the world. Enormous earth-moving machines, cranes and mountains of coal—not to mention toxic wastes and gaping scars—would cover the sacred mesa. Ancient wells were going dry as aquifers were emptied feeding a slurry that carried the mined coals miles away for processing. Roberta Blackgoat, a tribal elder, would remark sometime later that the tragedy had taken many of the lives of the traditional leaders both by suicide and alcoholism.

The postscript to this story signals the beginning of the end. The United Methodist Board of Church and Society was called upon by an organization of Big Mountain traditional leaders to help them seek justice. As general secretary of the board, the staff and I arranged for the spring 1998 visit of United Nations Special Rapporteur on Religious Intolerance, Abdelfattah Amor from Tunisia, with the approval of the United States government. Mr. Amor would gather the testimony of the traditional people on Black Mesa and elsewhere and report to the High Commission on Human Rights of the United Nations. Meeting at the Black Mesa home of Glenna Begay, an elder in the matriarchal Navajo Nation, two hundred traditional Hopi and Navajo gathered to greet Amor. There, he heard testimony charging that the federal laws had denied them access to water, legalized the confiscation of their livestock, prevented them from gathering firewood to heat their homes and improve them, as well as other human rights violations. Also, the operation of the Peabody Coal Company was exhausting the underground water table, polluting streams and destroyed burial grounds and sacred sites–over four thousand had been destroyed, according to the testimony. Others would plea for saving traditional ways and providing cultural education for the children.

An Arizona State University researcher, Annette Cedar said of the dilemma: "The1974 Relocation Law...was about the multinational mining and oil interests in the mineral-rich corridor of land which is sacred to the people who live here."[53] Another added that once Peabody is done, the petroleum and other energy companies will follow because there is oil and uranium here. The world community was already aware of these flagrant violations. These hearings would substantiate these claims and have an impact on future declarations made by European governments and, eventually, the mining of coal. In 2006, the Peabody Coal Company ceased mining coal on Black Mesa–but only for a short recess. Peabody is expected to resume its exploitation of the Black Mesa environment and the people who call that place sacred.

THE CONTINUING STORY

The story continues in endless repetition as Native territories are targeted by energy corporations to extract coal, oil, uranium and other wealth necessary to fuel the needs and greeds of modern society. Broken promises and violated treaties wrack poverty-stricken reservation citizens as their birthrights are violated and their way of life is compromised. The Lakota can no longer count on the Fort Laramie Treaty of 1868 to safeguard their territories as Peabody Coal, Kerr McGee and other companies open vast mining operations threatening the sacred place known as the Black Hills. The Federal Government has offered a settlement of millions of dollars for the Black Hills, a settlement that the Lakota have rejected. Further to the east at an earlier time, violating the promise of George Washington to leave the

Seneca Nation undisturbed, Kinzua Dam has flooded all of the Seneca traditional homelands and ancient graves forming "Lake Perfidy," where tourists now water and jet ski. There are too many examples to be included in this study and the weight of them continues to oppress an ancient race of people learning how to live in an alien culture where materialistic hungers consume the earth and its treasures.

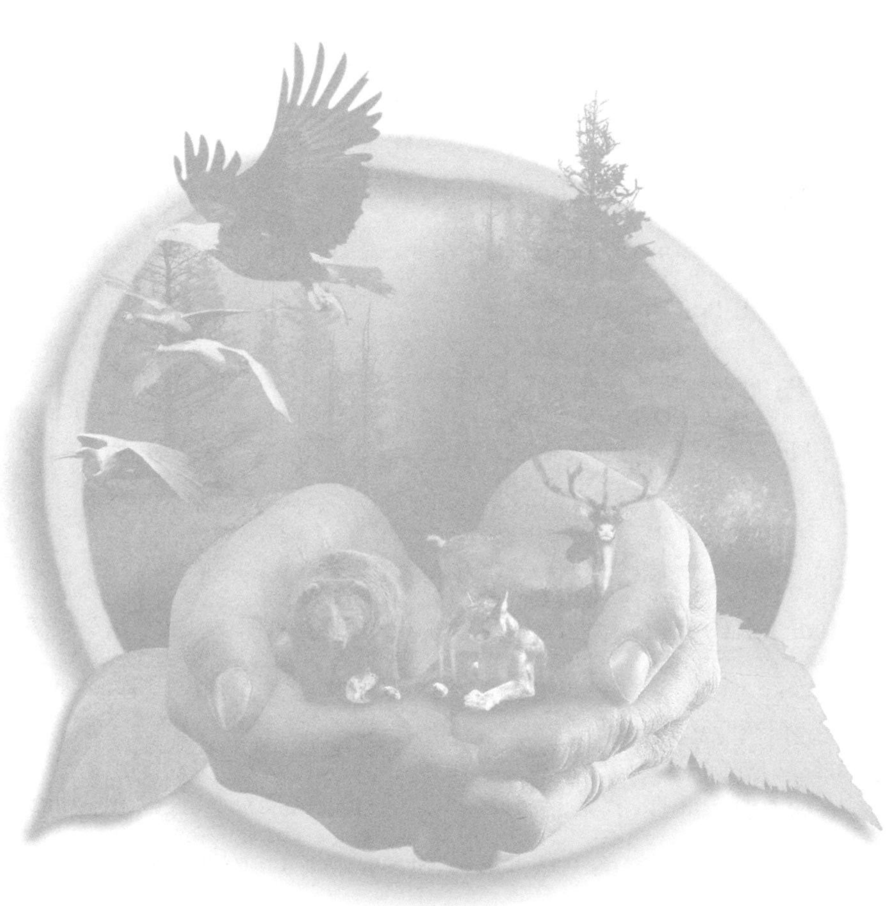

CHAPTER 7

The American Odyssey: Walking Together Toward Tomorrow

Felix Cohen, legal scholar of Indian law and history, said that Indians were the miner's canaries for American society. The multiple ills that are visited upon them are only a prelude and a harbinger of what is to be expected for society as a whole. Relatively few Americans today understand the "miner's canary" analogy. Nor do they understanding the consequences of Native peoples vanishing from the earth and the seemingly coincidental eradication of thousands of life forms as a dominant culture feeds its insatiable appetite for material prosperity. We see the original stewards of this continent estranged from the land as exploitative forces initiate measures so severe as to produce startling case histories of environmental degradation, economic instability and social disintegration. Judged by its actions, American society does not revere the earth as a living organism to be preserved for future generations of human beings. The earth is now a "resource" to American society, offering a stark contrast between a people who view the world as sacred and a people who do not. We have learned bitter lessons by separating the people from the land–it kills both.

People are like trees, and groups of people are like forests. While the forests are composed of many different kinds of trees, these trees intertwine their roots so strongly that it is impossible for the strongest winds that blow on our islands to uproot the forest, for each tree strengthens it neighbor, and their roots are inextricably entwined.

In the same way the people of our islands, composed of members of nations and races from all over the world, are beginning to intertwine their roots so strongly that no troubles will affect them. Just as one tree standing alone would soon be destroyed by the first strong wind which came along, so it is impossible for any person, any family or any community to stand alone against the troubles of this world.

— Haida Chief Skidegate, 1966

SURVIVAL OF THE EARTH

At one time it was estimated that American Indian herbal medicine practices were used in 90 percent of the American pharmacopeia (Western medicines). In its first meeting of the United Nations Permanent Indigenous Forum in 2002, Native people began drafting a resolution demanding the collective ownership of land and just payments for their medicinal knowledge used by drug companies from time immemorial without compensating Native peoples. Indian medicine people tell us today that many of the plants, herbs, mosses, barks and flowers used in traditional medicine no longer exist. They must seek new visions and dream new dreams to be led to other plant life that will supply their medical needs. Toxic waste dumps, uranium poisoning, destructive mining practices, fluorocarbon gases, destruction of the ozone shield protecting the earth from excessive doses of ultraviolet rays and disposable products are but a few of the threats that characterize our current dilemma. The litany of American ills reads badly and manifests itself in beer can-strewn highways and public landfills stuffed with the artifacts of a culture never celebrated in the spiritual ceremonies of Native peoples nor on the high altars of Western religions. Perhaps some truly do believe that all will be redeemed by the provocative blinking television image of Iron Eyes Cody (well-remembered Indian actor) tearfully standing in garbage as a crude commercial reminder of what the world once was and could be again–offered as a public service message squeezed between the evening news and late-night programming. Perhaps, after all, Iron Eyes Cody symbolizes spiritual despair in an age of material hope.

We have learned bitter lessons by separating the people from the land–it kills both.

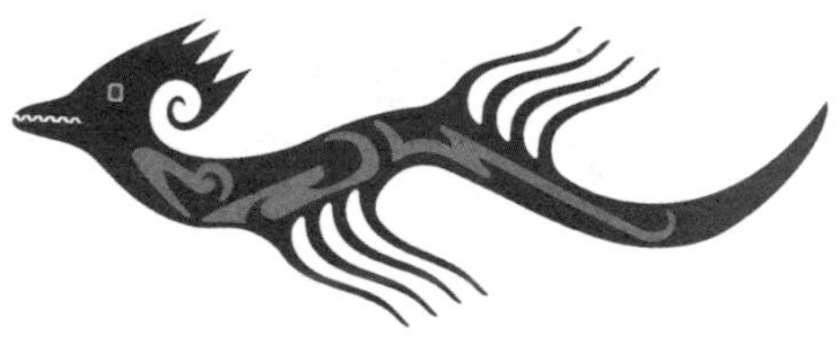

The litany of American ills reads badly and manifests itself in beer can-strewn highways and public landfills stuffed with the artifacts of a culture never celebrated in the spiritual ceremonies of Native peoples nor on the high altars of Western religions.

If the circle of life is to remain unbroken, the teachings of our Creator and the wisdom of our elders must pass from generation to generation. But America's circle is very small and does not embrace the sacredness of God's creation. America's circle cycles every two or four years–from one national election to the next–and would ruin the whole world to get from election to re-election. This seems to be the extent of the vision and it is accentuated by the focus of the television cameras and further detailed in "op-ed" pieces published in the *New York Times* or the *Washington Post.* We give thanks in our churches for the next world, having forgotten how to walk in a sacred manner in the present world.

Christians must speak a spiritual language quite different from the language of the politics of nation or state if we are to clearly identify with the images of love, justice and freedom that are central to the body of Christian teachings. Otherwise, these images will live simply as cherished theories of the Christian church. Understanding the analogy of the "miner's canary" is essential today as policics that oncc wcrc solely directed toward Native Americans are being exercised against other racial ethnic people. Racism in the United States finds its origin in materialistic acquisitiveness and expresses itself in the redefinition of rights and responsibilities that defy the intentions of the founding documents of the nation. It is clear that Native Americans, Hispanic/Latinos, African Americans and Asians are now often made the scapegoats of uneasy economies. Given the disturbing economic realties we are facing today with rising unemployment rates and the increasing national debt burden, it cannot but get worse.

"We do not inherit the earth from our ancestors, we borrow it from our children."

We have also come to learn that the same strategies employed to oppress Indians are now being used to oppress other racial ethnic people resulting in the loss of some basic rights. It wasn't until other racial ethnic people discovered toxic waste dumps—once targeted primarily for Indian lands—being sited in their neighborhoods, that the phrase "environmental racism" found its way into our conversations. It should be noted that American Indian people would also apply "environmental racism" to the disappearance of natural world "people" such as animals, fish, and trees as well.

Whatever its scholarly interpretation, the Gospel of John, in the first few verses of Chapter One, assures us that God made everything that is and reminds us that we are related not only to each other but to all that God created. That is, we are related

As indigenous spirituality in both its traditional and Christian forms finds new expression on the earth and ancient prophecies become the reality of the day, we must adopt a new planetary perspective...

to everything that exists. Of course, it is quite easy for us to understand how we are related to each other as human beings, but so much more difficult for us to comprehend that we are also related to other life forms also made by God. Being related means that we care for those entities as family. In Matthew 6:25-32, we hear Jesus' teachings about the loving parenting of God in caring for all of creation. God feeds the birds and clothes the lilies and grass of the fields. In the third chapter of John, wc rcad, "For God so loved the world that God gave his only Son, that whoever believed in him should not perish but have eternal life. For God sent the Son into the world, not to condemn the world, but that the world might be saved through God." This saving of the world must be understood as God's continuing work through us–we who have committed ourselves to the work of salvation in our faith commitments to the living Word. The world, then, is the object of this salvation and not only we ourselves as human beings. As indigenous spirituality in both its traditional and Christian forms finds new expression on the earth and ancient prophecies become the reality of the day, we must adopt a new planetary perspective–even as we look to the colonizing of interstellar space seeking a future cosmic "lifeboat." We must accept responsibility for adopting a spiritually wise, technologically sound, ethical and farsighted stewardship of the planet and a renewed respect for nature on which all life depends, remembering the American Indian saying, "We do not inherit the earth from our ancestors, we borrow it from our children."

INDIAN GAMBLING

It is safe to say that The United Methodist Church has been as responsible as any church for preventing the growth of gambling throughout the United States. We now face a dilemma of conflicting policies, supporting Native American sovereignty on the one hand and opposing gambling on the other. The issue is disruptive and divisive to church people. The issue divides Indian country, too. Although gambling is often found in the historical cultural practices and celebrations of Native cultures, some nations, such as the Six Nations Iroquois, have strict prohibitions against it. These disagreements have caused suffering in families, brought brother to blows against brother, pitted sister against sister and divided churches and communities.

In 1979, the Seminole of south Florida opened its first bingo hall. Less than a decade later, fifty tribes had opened bingo halls producing more than $250 million annually. The Supreme Court later ruled that the states could not interfere with this new form of economic development. With the outbreak of casino gambling, earnings are now closing in on $10 billion. About ten percent of those tribes attempting to establish gambling revenues have succeeded. Still, Native people continue to be the poorest population in the United States. It is estimated by the Native American Rights Fund that even if the proceeds from Indian gambling were distributed equally to all Indians in the United States with each person receiving $3,000, it would not significantly raise Indian per-capita income significantly above the current level of $4,500. Tribes are required by law to enter into gambling compacts with the respective states in which they are located.

While the early stages of Indian gaming were fraught with criminal takeovers or outright theft by outside managers, it wasn't long before the experience became a crash course in business management for a people who had never engaged in such fast-track operations. One of the most successful examples of Indian gaming is to be found in the Oneida Nation of Wisconsin. Under the leadership of tribal chair, Debbie Doxtater, a United Methodist, the tribe determined that their casino gaming revenues would be spent buying back lost lands, rebuilding the reservation infrastructure, establishing senior housing and health care facilities, addressing educational needs and establishing their own bank. Their plan also intentionally visualized less dependence on gaming while diversifying their economic base with other businesses. The Oneidas are substantially on track with their plan and they provide a remarkable model for programs derived from gambling that benefit the tribe.

Some years ago, I was asked by the New England Conference to debate the manager of Foxwoods, the largest Indian casino in the United States, if not the largest casino in the world. The white community was upset with proposed plans for the expansion of Indian gaming in New England and the church was at the center of the discussion. The manager of the casino and I spent much time–he, explaining the need for tribal economic development through gaming and I, articulating both the strong positions of The United Methodist Church in matters of Indian sovereignty and its opposition to gambling. After stating that we would support the Prince of Monaco and the claims of his nation **as a sovereign nation state**, I explained that we would not endorse gambling as a means of supporting their national economy. However, because we recognized Monaco's sovereignty, we also supported their need to develop their economy even though we did not agree with their method of doing so. Such is the conflict among well-reasoned people. My final rhetorical question perhaps captured a notion that the audience was not prepared to answer. "Why is it, just now, that you have come to oppose gambling in organized public meetings," I asked. "Where were you when the Roman Catholics played bingo in their fellowship halls? Where were you when the volunteer firefighters had Monte Carlo night in their fund-raising carnivals?" A discussion ensued about the lack of land base and issues of economic development, treaty rights and sovereignty and government deals that rendered Native Americans economically helpless in New England. Such conversations can be held all over the country where there are tribal organizations preparing to launch gaming activities.

The National Indian Gaming Association

Created by Congress, the National Indian Gaming Association is an organization of more than 120 Indian nations providing oversight for Indian gaming in the United States. One of their responsibilities is to provide a buffer between the states and Indian gaming tribes. With the promise of casino "cash cows," the states have increasingly sought to tax the revenues of gaming tribes and gain more regulatory control. In many cases, states benefit from large multi-million allotments flowing voluntarily from gaming tribes. Like it or not, we must realize that Indian gaming is often the only source of employment and revenues available to tribes. The earnings are used for subsistence, cultural preservation and survival. With Indian unemployment three to four times higher than the national average and reservation unemployment ranging from 50 to 85 percent, the gambling tide will not soon be turned back.

INDIAN HEALTH

In their 2001 testimony on appropriations for the Indian Health Service, the Friends Committee on National Legislation cited a critical study by the Harvard School of Public Health/ Centers for Disease Control and Prevention. Their report is chilling. American Indian/Alaska Natives have the lowest life

expectancies in this country, or in any nation in this hemisphere except Haiti. Indian people suffer disproportionately higher morbidity/mortality rates than all U.S. populations. Alcoholism is 950 percent greater; tuberculosis is 630 percent greater; diabetes is 350 percent greater; unintentional injury is 270 percent greater; suicide is 70 percent greater (while one in ten youth in the United States attempt suicide, one in ten in Indian country succeeds); pneumonia and influenza is 61 percent greater; and homicide is 60 percent greater. Again, the Friends Committee reports that the death rate attributed to alcohol for Native Americans seven times higher than that of the general U.S. population. HIV/AIDS infection is epidemic in some Indian communities and, according to Ray Buckley of United Methodist Communications, Native gangs are growing rapidly. This is evident by the shocking statistics in Navajo country where the per-capita homicide rate is the highest in the United States.

"The United Methodist Church (and its predecessor bodies) has sinned and continues to sin against its Native American brothers and sisters and offers this formal apology for it participation, intended and unintended, in the violent colonization of their land."

A SEASON OF APOLOGIES

The Christian churches in the United States have been pushed and pulled into a new era of enlightenment, recognizing their role in the subjugation of America's Native people. In its General Conference in 1992 and again in 2004, The United Methodist Church declared: "The United Methodist Church (and its predecessor bodies) has sinned and continues to sin against its Native American brothers and sisters and offers this formal apology for it participation, intended and unintended, in the violent colonization of their land." It further affirmed upholding the American Indian Religious Freedom Act; access to and protection of sacred sites and public lands for ceremonial purposes; the use of religious symbols (feathers, tobacco, sweet grass, bones, and so forth); and recommended that local churches develop similar statements of confession.

In the late 1980s and 1990s, the Christian church had already begun to express its regrets to Native peoples. Pope Paul II apologized and called for reconciliation, expressing regret for the overzealous past conduct of Jesuits and the oppression experienced at the hands of cruel colonizers. Churches in the Northwest issued apologies to Native Americans and committed themselves to helping to protect spiritual traditions. The United Church of Christ traveled to Hawaii to apologize for the destructive work of the Congregationalist Churches as they descended on the Native Islands following Captain Cook's voyages, destroying the Natives and their culture. Other mainline churches followed suit. Today, most have adopted policies that support Native causes, cultural lifestyles, economic development and religious freedom.

RACIAL STEREOTYPING

American Indian racial stereotyping has been a strong issue in the mainline denominations, including The United Methodist Church. Specifically, the opposition to Native American sports images and mascots has gained wide attention and is still on the agenda of national church staff today. Native American stereotyping in the sports world offers one of the most blatant and overt expressions of racism allowed to exist unchecked in the United States. While there are non-racist mascots such as the Navy Goat, the Army Mule and the Yale Bulldog, there are also racist Indian mascots, such as the grotesque big-nosed Chief Wahoo of the Cleveland Indians and Chief Noc-A-Homa of the Atlanta Braves that continue to dehumanize Native Americans. Suits are still pending against the trademark use of the Washington Redskins. There are still large numbers of

Little noted by the 2004 General Conference was the 1996 apology and the embarrassing slight offered to the Cheyenne Nation for the massacre at Sand Creek and at a village of Cheyenne Indians in Colorado Territory by Colonel John Chivington. Chivington was an elder in the Methodist Church serving as a minister in Ohio where he also spent a term as a district superintendent. Working his way westward, he became the presiding elder of the First Methodist Episcopal Church in Denver. There, he was offered a chaplain's commission in the First Colorado Volunteer Regiment. Instead, he asked for a fighting commission. An experienced military officer, he savored the opportunity to fight Indians. In November of 1864, he got his opportunity. As part of the ongoing opposition to Indian presence, a plan was devised to attack the village of well- known Cheyenne leader Black Kettle. Declaring that it was honorable to use any means under God's heaven to kill Indians, Chivington instructed his troops to "kill and scalp all, big and little; nits make lice." They attacked the Cheyenne village with a vengeance, killing some 500 of the possibly 700 Indians in the camp–most of them old men, women and children.

In the 1996 General Conference, arrangements had been made for the chief of the Cheyenne Nation, Lawrence Hart, to be present to receive the apology of the church. Upon its adoption, the presiding bishop called upon the chief to make a response to the conference. As Chief Hart stood to address the conference, the presiding bishop observed that it was noon and lunch was the order of the day. The conference was immediately recessed and the chief was never able to speak to the United Methodist Church assembled in its General Conference.

colleges and high schools that use Native American characters or mascots to symbolize their sports teams. Whenever the appropriate agencies of the church challenge these schools or question the projected location of the next General Conference because of practices of racial stereotyping, there is usually grass-roots opposition to the implementation of the church's own policies.

...even today, young Indian children often believe the Hollywood stereotypes of their own people.

Movies have not done much better. Earlier black and white films as well as more recent giant-screen movies reinforce the themes of Manifest Destiny and the notion that Indian conquest and westward settlement was God's idea. From 1908 to the 1950s, Indians were portrayed as "bloodthirsty Redskins," the ultimate enemy, the savage murderer of women and children. They rode horses, wore headdresses, killed buffalo with bows and arrows, scalped white people and put them to death by tomahawk. These images established stereotypes that continue to influence perceptions of Native Americans today. It will take generations to eradicate these images while even today, young Indian children often believe the Hollywood stereotypes of their own people. The advent of television further popularized these images in serials and repeated broadcasts. It wasn't until the 1970s that a different interpretation of Indians and Native culture appeared on the silver screen and on television. It was about this time that real Indians were included in the acting casts and we saw a new genre of movie in "Tell Them Willie Boy is Here," "Little Big Man," "A Man Called Horse," "Billy Jack," and "I Heard the Owl Call My Name." Today, we can watch films such as "Dances With Wolves," with reasonable certainty that there is care taken to employ Indian actors and faithfully reflect a truer depiction of the cultural practices of Native Americans.

SOON AND VERY SOON

The hymn by Andrae' Crouch, "Soon and Very Soon," may well be the theme song for the church's efforts on behalf of Native Americans. While the program agencies of the church are, in some cases, diligently following Indian legislation in the Congress and in the states, the church at large is often unaware of issues challenging the survival of Native people today. In fact, even in states with relatively large Indian populations,the church is generally not in touch with Indian communities either on or off of the reservations–one obvious exception being the Oklahoma Indian Missionary Conference. This behavior has not changed a great deal since 1976 when the Ethnic Minority Local Church (EMLC) priority was inaugurated by the General Conference of The United Methodist Church. Recognizing the racist trends in the church and genuinely seeking ways to intentionally establish and nurture racial ethnic congregations, this program continued to be renewed each General Conference for many quadrennia. However, the EMLC priority did not have a visible effect on Native church communities.

In one Western annual conference where I traveled as a national agency staff person with the General Board of Church and Society, even after two years of EMLC programming in the denomination, this conference had done nothing. Not only had they made no plans for ethnic minority local church programming, they had not asked for a dollar from the local churches to help implement plans should they be adopted. In conversations with superintendents and staff in the conference office, I was told they did not have significant racial ethnic people in their conference to motivate programming. I observed that the conference was established in the middle of Native American territories and they were surrounded by Native nations on every point of the compass with whom they had lived for 150 years. We began to work on the means by which the conference and its local churches could develop plans to be in dialogue with Native peoples and get a better understanding of how the churches could respond more authentically to Native issues. Eventually, plans were developed to dialogue with Native communities and some programs came out of it. Before I left the meeting, I passed a hat in which we contributed the first EMLC dollars for that conference.

...many conferences are oblivious to the fact that Indian populations exist in every annual conference.

This story is told as an example of a typical response characterizing not only an earlier era of racial-ethnic local church work by the denomination but, more specifically, how previously ineffective programs necessitated the United Methodist Native American Comprehensive Plan. After the church established this plan in 1988, it was quickly followed by special African American, Asian and Hispanic/Latino church projects designed to invigorate established racial-ethnic ministries and stimulate new ones. While they continue as denominational priorities, The United Methodist Church has generally moved these programs into the general boards and agencies of the church without additional funding from the General Conference. Already financially strapped agencies were required to allocate funds from other ministries to fund these efforts.

Today, working within the General Board of Global Ministries, the Native American Comprehensive Plan (NACP) and its board directs efforts to expand congregational development of local Native American churches. NACP provides leadership training to strengthen Native effectiveness in recruitment and ministry in local churches and conferences among lay persons and clergy. Native schools for lay speaking and evangelism, the development of culturally relevant ministries with Native young adults, youth camps, family camp ministries and training for annual conference Committees on Native American Ministries are some of the signature programs of NACP.

Many conferences are still not aware that they are required by *The Discipline of The United Methodist Church* to establish Committees on Native American Ministries to formulate new Native church ministries and administer the expenditure of 50 percent of the retained Native American Ministries Sunday offerings for Native ministries in the conferences. In fact, many conferences are oblivious to the fact that Indian populations exist in every annual conference. Complimenting this important ministry is the National United Methodist Native American Center that addresses Indian education and the recruitment and training of Native American persons for ministry in the church. Additionally, the Native American International Caucus focuses on church issues associated with Native American survival, effective church ministries among Native people and monitors justice issues in a national context. Probably the most effective jurisdictional Indian ministry is the Southeastern Jurisdiction Agency for Native American Ministries, with headquarters at Lake Junaluska, North Carolina. They have a relationship with every annual conference of the Southeast Jurisdiction.

As Christianity becomes a minority religion in America, we must find new means of expressing our historical creeds that do not so much create great expectations of others as inspire faithful expectations of ourselves.

But all of this is happening within the church. What about our relationships with the large population of Indians who have no relationship with the church (fewer than 10 percent) and may never feel safe within its walls? Will we be as zealous in supporting the critical and controversial issues of Native survival when they have no direct relationship with the church? Will our pleas for forgiveness bring about changed behavior, new relationships and new self-understanding as well as individual, personal atonement? Or are we simply perpetuating the colonial spirit of Manifest Destiny, concerned only with making Indians into productive, well-behaved citizens of the United States? As Christianity becomes a minority religion in America, we must find new means of expressing our historical creeds that do not so much create great expectations of others as inspire faithful expectations of ourselves. We cannot allow guilt to paralyze us while merely articulating sound policies that create the illusion of action. Without active engagement in the issues that may frighten us, we cannot fulfill the promises we have embraced in a Gospel loaded with verbs.

TOWARD TOMORROW

We cannot allow guilt to paralyze us while merely articulating sound policies that create the illusion of action. Without active engagement in these issues that may frighten us, we cannot fulfill the promises we have embraced in a Gospel loaded with verbs.

Denominational apologies to American Indians are a good place for the church to continue its walk with Indian societies in the United States. The church can play a powerful role in the survival of Native peoples. The formation of old-fashioned "study groups," the writing of new educational curriculum and significant financial commitments will help to shore up the support necessary to ensure the ongoing viability of a unique people in a unique democratic system. Only a strong and unified voice will shout down the oppressive forces determined to exterminate a race of people. The church is in a unique position to accomplish this. How do we deal with our own self-interests when confronted by tribal efforts of the Lac du Flambeau Chippewa band for control of water quality in Wisconsin, when it is opposed by the state Department of Natural Resources? How do we assist the Ramapouge Mountain Indians in their claim against the Ford Motor Company, charging that the company created one of the most toxic landfills in the United States on Indian territory? How do we support the Western Shoshone Nation in their continuing efforts for a just settlement of their lands? Keep Urban Indian Health Care program funds from being slashed by the Federal

Government? Protect Native arts and crafts from massive imports of Asian forgeries? Prevent Washington lobbyists from victimizing Indian economies and self-development? Restrain administrations in Washington from dumping yet more nuclear waste on the sacred Yucca Mountain site? Prevent Indian burial cites and sacred places from being destroyed and exploited for commercial interests? Work with Indian communities to reduce alcoholism and substance abuse? The list is long and it will grow as Indian leadership seek partnerships to address these life and death issues.

The church is uniquely suited to work with Native communities both in the cities and on the reservations to achieve health and wholeness. The key is to plug into the sources of information. For this, we must be directly in communication with Indian tribes or entities. If you are in an urban area, look for a Native American Center in your area. If you are not close to an Indian population base, get on the mailing lists of the National Congress of American Indians in Washington D.C., the Native American Rights Fund in Boulder Colorado, or the Indian Law Resource Center, Helena, Montana. There are large numbers of Indian organizations working in every state that can provide direction for church and secular groups who are interested in addressing state and federal legislation or policies for administering Indian programs or services. Certainly the Bureau of Indian Affairs in Washington D.C. is likely to yield a rich harvest of information. Another resource is the United Nations Permanent Forum on Indigenous Peoples, an entity that has taken Native peoples years to form and an equally long time to gain recognition by the United Nations.

Only a strong and unified voice will shout down the oppressive forces determined to exterminate a race of people.

The litany of Indian issues and their numbers should not deter us from a faithful response to critical issues. We must decide

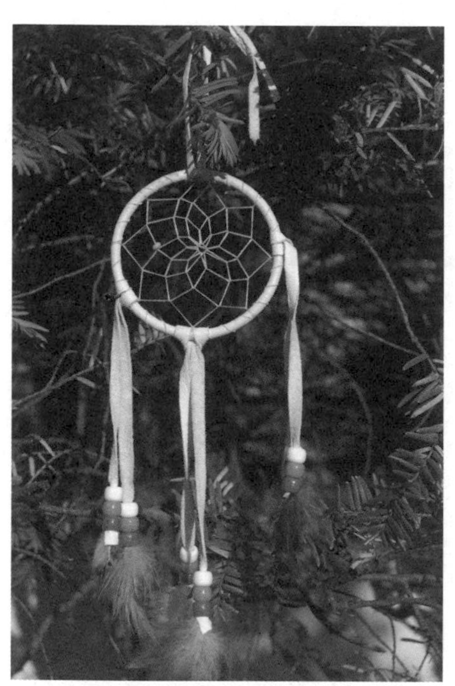

what is realistically possible and take on a project that seems to be proportionate to our abilities. Soon we will learn to take on more and it will not be long before we are caught up in these justice issues that will be carried out in association with Indian people and represent a substantial commitment of our time and resources. Standing in solidarity with American Indian people is best expressed by the church and its men and women through working relationships with real Indian groups and through gathering support for their self-identified struggles and goals. In every case, church actions of support must be authentic, informed and able to sustain long-term involvement with the issues and with Indian people.

In January of 1990, our Native American tribal and spiritual leaders traveled to Moscow, Russia to consider the survival of Native peoples. Their report and their challenge to us can be found in this joint statement:

> "We have jeopardized the future of our coming generations with our greed and lust for power. The warnings are clear and time is now a factor…We speak of our children, yet we savage the spawning beds of the salmon and herring, and kill the whale in his home. We advance through the forests of the earth felling our rooted brothers indiscriminately, leaving no seeds for the future. We exploit the land and resources of the poor and indigenous peoples of the world. We have become giants, giants of destruction and now we have gathered here to acknowledge this and to see what we must do to change… Indigenous peoples possess many different habits and lifestyles but all recognize they are children of Mother Earth and that we receive from Her our life, our health, the air we breathe, the water we drink, our everyday food, and our energy. Earth suffers ill treatment because of lack of respect. All of us can

understand the importance of the health of Mother Earth and all have a potential to enjoy our lives in greater harmony with the forces which create life. Brothers and sisters, we must return to the spiritual values that are the foundation of life. We must love and respect all living things, have compassion for the poor and the sick, respect and understanding for the women and female life on this Earth who bear the sacred gift of life. We must return to the prayers, ceremonies, meditations, rituals and celebrations of thanksgiving which link us with the spiritual powers that sustain us and, by example, teach our children to respect"[54]

Finally, if the church is to remain a viable moral force within modern society, it must grasp the significance of the past and the unfolding demands of the future. Nothing epitomizes this more dramatically than our relationship with the survival of American Indians. What would we tell Red Jacket today if we lived beside him and attended the churches around him? If we took Native spirituality seriously, would the great Native prayers of thanksgiving change our approach to the Sacrament of Communion, or alert us to the feel of the earth under our feet or the movement of other life forms about us? If Indians are the miner's canary for civilization, how much time do we have to understand the "groaning of creation," and notice the narrow precipice of life on which we travel? If the church takes seriously its historic confessions, it will suffer with the oppressed and reject the materialistic values that are anathema to our own survival. Only when we understand that spirituality is the highest form of political consciousness and make decisions for ourselves and our children that consider their impact on the next seven generations, will we be able to embrace the spirit and freedom of the Gospel.

What would we tell Red Jacket today if we lived beside him and attended churches around him? If we took Native spirituality seriously, would the great Native prayers of thanksgiving change our approach to the Sacrament of Communion, or alert us to the feel of the earth under our feet or the movement of other life forms about us?

How does the unique historic expression of Christian sacred values make room for the spiritual yearnings of other special peoples? Native American spiritual practices and faithfulness to ancient traditions rest on understandings that are not alien to the Christian experience. Our challenge as Christians is to understand why our expressions of sacred value may be alien to indigenous peoples. Understanding our history and Christianity's current cultural obligations will provide us with insights that may eventually free us to become the people we were meant to be when God created us.

We have always understood universal wisdom through the common elements of our everyday lives. Native teachings have passed from generation to generation and continue to be shared as we try to make sense of a now calamitous social environment. As God spoke to our ancient relatives, God speaks to us today through our faith. The wisdom we learn brings balance to life. When we lose the wisdom of what we are to be on this earth and what it means to live in harmony, we destroy the purpose of creation. We gain understanding through love and respect for one another and the living creation. Respect begins with reverence for God–the life that is within all things. And because all things are created by God, all are relatives and must be treated as family. Their health is our health. Our health is their health. God's circle of creation must not be broken, for it symbolizes perfection, equality, unity, life and eternity. With Job, we watch for the morning stars singing together and all people of God shouting for joy. We open our minds and spirits to yet another vision that will bring the Great Mystery, Wakan Tonka, the Great Spirit, Yahweh, Elohim, the Lord God, closer to the lives of the people.

Because of our theological concepts of wholeness and community, unity and family (in all of its contexts), we remain a sovereign people celebrating the sovereignty of God in our lives in spite of historical efforts to separate us from our rich theology. Over 200 rich languages still intone sacred melodies and voice God's presence in our churches, halls and homes. Our Indian hymns still inspire the people as we sing of the ministry of Jesus in our churches, camps, tents and Chickees. We witness to the availability of the Word to all persons without condition in any place and time. We do not insist that one recognize God in a particular way, in a specific time and an identifiable place. The teachings of Jesus free us from confinement as we recognize

God at work in all things everywhere. While humankind may loose destructive forces upon the face of the earth, God stands ready to love us unconditionally.

The sacred instructions given to our people by God to revere and preserve in ancient times have been renewed and revitalized in Jesus and the New Covenant. Love, grace and forgiveness bring healing and gentleness to the human community as clear signs of a New Promise. Indian pastors, theologians and church leaders in The United Methodist Church have an opportunity to hold the mirror into which Western civilization can peer to see its own reflection and to catch a glimpse of a new vision of creation and the unity of God. Does not the history of our people teach us of the power of the Holy Spirit?

Indian pastors, theologians and church leaders in the United Methodist Church have an opportunity to hold the mirror into which Western civilization can peer to see it own reflection and to catch a glimpse of a new vision of creation and the unity of God.

We have been in preparation since ancient times to carry this loving ministry and to move among the people of the earth. We who live in two cultures and those claiming historic Christian creeds need to affirm this ministry and reinforce our commitment to speak clearly and prophetically on behalf of the dispossessed, the hungry, the naked, the sick, the imprisoned, the poor, the oppressed and all living creatures who have no voice.

NOTES & REFERENCES

Introduction

1. Although commonly used by Indian authors and others, this reference can be found in Benjamin Keen (translator), *The Life of Christopher Columbus by his Son Ferdinand* (Greenwood Press, New York, 1978).
2. The Seneca and Cayuga were two of the original Five Nations (Haudenosaunee) of the Iroquois Confederacy. Later, the Tuscarora Nation would join the confederacy to form the Six Nations. The French called this confederacy the "Iroquois," while the English called them thc "Six Nations."
3. The Northwest Ordinance, Article III, 1787. The entire text can be found in *The Annals of America* (The Encyclopedia Britannica, Inc.1976).
4. As quoted in *American Indian Policy Review Commission: Final Report*, (U.S. Government Printing Office, Washington, D.C., 1977).

First Word

5. *Are We Giving America Back to the Indians?* Interstate Congress for Equal Rights and Responsibilities (Winner, South Dakota, 1976).
6. Jack Weatherford, *Indian Givers* (Fawcett Columbine, New York, 1988).

Chapter 1

7. *A Basic Call to Consciousness, The Hau de no sau nee Address to the Western World* (Geneva, Switzerland, 1977), p. 12.
8. Peter Nabokov, ed., *Native American Testimony* (Harper and Row, New York 1978), p. 108.
9. Norris Handley, ed., *The American Indian: Essays from Pacific Historical Review* (Santa Barbara, Clio Press, 1974), p. 101.
10. As retold from a narrative written by Martha E. Baker, Northern California Education Project (Public Domain, 1973).
11. Red Jacket, a Seneca Chief whose reserve was located on Buffalo Creek, now Buffalo, New York.
12. Oren Lyons, a Faithkeeper of the Onondaga Nation.
13. The United States Bureau of Census officially counts around four million Native people. Native nations and organizations are well aware that this is an inaccurate count and the Bureau of Census acknowledges it as well (vis-a-vis a conversation between Thom White Wolf Fassett

and Dr. Martha Farnsworth Richie, then Director, U. S. Bureau of the Census in Copenhagen, March, 1995). In reality, Native sources would number today's Native population at around ten million.

14. Henry F. Dobyns, *Native American Historical Demography*, the Newberry Library Center for the History of the American Indian Bibliographical Series (Indiana University Press, Bloomington, 1976).
15. This author met with James Michener in Alaska while he was writing his great tome on Alaska's formation and history published in 1988. Our conversations centered on the "land bridge" theory and Native American's own cosmology and understanding of their origins in the Americas that essentially rejected the theory. While it may be true that certain modern Inuit Circumpolar peoples traveled across a land bridge some time ago, the tribes and nations of America had a much more ancient history that did not link to a "land bridge" arrival concept. After sharing some of my writings and those of Indian friends and other Native sources, Michener wrote to me from the University of Texas, Austin, informing me that perhaps I would be happy to learn that he had rewritten his introduction to Alaska, acknowledging that there were other theories and origin stories repeated by Native nations that rejected the land bridge idea.
16. Supreme Court Justice William Douglas wrote a minority opinion in the case of *Sierra Club v. Morton* which declared that Nature has the right to be defended as though it were a human being.
17. Paul LeJeune, *The Jesuit Relations and Allied Documents: Travels and Explorations of the Jesuit Missionaries in New France*, 1610-1791 (Relation for the year 1634, Reuben Gold Thwaites, ed., Cleveland, 1889-1901), Vol. 18, pp. 105-107.

Chapter 2

18. *Respecting an Attempt to Evangelize the Heathen* (London: British Missionary Society, 1795) Fassett Collection.
19. Ibid.
20. Charles C. Mann, 1491 (Alfred A. Knopf, New York, 2005), p. 335.
21. Ibid., p. 331.
22. Ibid.

23. Ibid., p.333.
24. Traditional Seneca memory. However, the entire text of Red Jacket's speech can be found in *The Annals of America* (Encyclopedia Britannica, Inc., 1976) Volume 4, pp. 194-196.
25. Manuscript, "Statement of Facts" (ca 1814), Fassett Collection.
26. See 31 U. S. C. (6 Pet.) 515, 559-61, (1832).

Chapter 3

27. John D. Lang, Samuel Taylor, Jr., *Report of a Visit to Some of the Tribes of Indians Located West of the Mississippi River* (New York, 1843, Fassett Collection), p. 7.
28. Ibid., p. 28.
29. Ibid., p. 31.
30. Frederick Webb Hodges, ed., *Handbook of American Indians* (Bureau of Ethnology, Bulletin 30, Part I, Washington, D.C.), p. 97.
31. *The Doctrines and Discipline of the Methodist Episcopal Church* (New York, 1848), pp. 183-184.
32. 41 Congress, 3rd Session, Congressional Globe, p. 743.
33. Ibid, pp. 1112, 1578, 1758.

Chapter 4

34. USC Title 8, Section 1401 (a) (2).
35. Lewis Meriam, ed., *The Problem of Indian Administration* (Johns Hopkins Press, Baltimore, 1928).
36. Ibid., p. 7.
37. Theodore W. Taylor, *The States and Their Indian Citizens* (United States Department of Interior, Bureau of Indian Affairs, Washington, DC, 1972), pp. 22-24.
38. John Collier, "Introduction," in Oliver La Farge, ed., *The Changing Indian* (University of Oklahoma Press, Norman, 1942) pp. 3-10.
39. John Collier, "Return to Dishonor," *Frontier*, (June 1954), pp. 8-9.
40. Ibid.
41. *The Spirit They Live In* (American Friends Service Committee, Philadelphia, 1956), pp. 12-13.

42. Bureau of Indian Affairs, "Statement on Current Issues in Indian Affairs," (April, 1956), pp. 1-3.

Chapter 5

43. "NARF Legal Review," (Native American Rights Fund, Boulder, Colorado Summer 1985), p. 8.
44. Special Message on "The Forgotten American" by President Johnson to the Senate on March 6, 1968, p. 2.
45. Message from the President of the United States, 1970, "Recommendations for Indian Policy" (U.S. Government Printing Office, Washington, D.C.).
46. Special Message of the President of the United Stated Richard M. Nixon to the Congress, from the White House, July 8, 1970.
47. Meriam Report, p. 51.
48. Lloyd Meeds, dissent. Congress of the United States, American Indian Policy Review Commission Final Report, 1977.
49. "The United Methodist Church and the American Indian (Native Americans)", adopted 1976.
50. "The United Methodist Church and America's Native People," *The Book of Resolutions* (The United Methodist Church General Conference, 1980).
51. *Native American Testimony*, p. 405.

Chapter 6

52. American Indian Policy Review Commission, Final Report.
53. Testimony received by the United Nations Rapporteur in Religious Tolerance Abdelfattah Amor in a 1998 report to the United Nations.

Chapter 7

54. A partial quote from the "Statement of Indigenous Delegates to the Global Forum on Environment and Development for Survival," Forum paper, (Moscow, January 15-19, 1990). See *Indigenous Economics, Toward a Natural World Order* (Ithaca, NY, Akwekon Journal, 1992) pp. 106-107, for complete text of Indigenous delegates.

BIBLIOGRAPHY

This short bibliography lists only the most essential readings that will compliment this study. While there are vast resources available examining the culture, history and religions of Native Americans, the references that follow serve as primers for the exploring reader and, in many cases, a wider exposure to those who wish to continue this study beyond the current goals of this work. Although many of these have an earlier publishing date, most have been reissued in subsequent printings.

All Roads are Good: Native Voices on Life and Culture. Washington, D.C.: Smithsonian Institution Press, 1994.

Allen, Paula Gunn. *The Sacred Hoop: Recovering the Feminine in American Indian Traditions*. Boston: Beacon Press, 1986.

Brown, Dee. *Bury My Heart at Wounded Knee*. New York: Bantam books, 1972.

Brown, Joseph Epes. *The Sacred Pipe*. New York: Penguin Books, 1971.

________________. *The Spiritual Legacy of the American Indian*. New York: Crossroad, 1982.

Deloria, Jr., Vine. *God Is Red* (2nd edition). Golden, Colorado: Fulcrum Publishing, 1992. A critically important work by a Native American scholar dealing with Native American spirituality and important environmental issues.

_____________. *The Indian Affair*. New York: Friendship Press, 1974.

_____________. *Custer Died for Your Sins*. New York: Avon Books, 1970.

_____________. *American Indians, American Justice*. Texas: University of Texas Press, 1983.

Eastman, Charles A. *The Soul of the Indian*. Nebraska: University of Nebraska Press, 1980.

Ewen, Alexander (ed.). *Voice of Indigenous Peoples: Native People Address the United Nations.* Santa Fe: Clear Light Publishers, 1994.
Survey of Native Nations voices covering contemporary and historical issues.

Gill, Sam D., and Irene F. Sullivan. *Dictionary of Native American Mythology.* New York: Oxford University Press, 1992.

Graymont, Barbara. *The Iroquois in the American Revolution.* Syracuse: Syracuse University Press, 1968.

Grinde, Jr., Donald, and Bruce E. Johansen. *Ecocide of Native America: Environmental Destruction of Indian Lands and Peoples.* Santa Fe: Clear Light, 1995).

Harrod, Howard L. *Mission Among the Blackfeet.* Oklahoma: University of Oklahoma Press, 1971.

Highwater, Jamake. *Native Land.* New York: Barnes & Noble Books, 1986.

Hirschfelder, Arlene and Paulette Molin. *The Encyclopedia of Native American Religions.* New York: MJF Books, 1992.

Jaimes, M. Annette (ed.). *The State of Native America.*Boston: South End Press, 1992).
Collection of essays on a wide variety of contemporary Native issues.

Jennings, Francis. *The Ambiguous Iroquois Empire.* New York: W. W. Norton & Co., 1984).

_____________. *The Invasion of America.* New York: W. W. Norton & Company, 1975.

Josephy, Jr., Alvin. *The Indian Heritage of America.* New York: Alfred A. Knopf, 1968.

Kidwell, Clara Sue, Homer Noley, George E. Tinker. *A Native American Theology*. New York: Orbis Books, 2001.

Lame Deer, John Fire, and Richard Erdoes. *Lame Deer, Seeker of Visions: The Life of a Sioux Medicine Man*. New York: Touchstone, 1972.
An excellent primer in Native American spirituality.

McGaa, Ed, Eagle Man. *Mother Earth Spirituality: Native American Paths to Healing Ourselves and Our World*. San Francisco: Harper San Francisco, 1990.

McGaa, Ed. *Native Wisdom*. Minneapolis: Four Directions Publishing, 1995.

Momaday, N. Scott. *House Made of Dawn*. New York: Harper, 1968.

Neihardt, John G. *Black Elk Speaks*, (8th printing). New York: Pocket Books, 1975.

Noley, Homer. *First White Frost: Native Americans and United Methodism*. Nashville: Abingdon, 1991.

Pritzker, Barry M. A *Native American Encyclopedia*. New York: Oxford University Press, 2000.

Riddle, Paxton. *The Education of Ruby Loonfoot*. Thorndike Press, 2003.
A United Methodist writer and an award winning fictional work.

Sams, Jamie and Twylah Nitsch. *Other Council Fires Were Here Before Ours*. New York: Harper Collins Publishers, 1991.

Steiger, Brad. *Indian Medicine Power*. Atglen, PA: Whitford Press, 1984.

Steiner, Stan. *The New Indians*. New York: Harper and Row, 1968.

Tinker, George. *Missionary Conquest: The Gospel and Native American Cultural Genocide*. Minneapolis: Fortress Press, 1993.

Underhill, Ruth M. *Red Man's America*. Chicago: The University of Chicago Press, 1953.

Weaver, Jace (ed.). *Defending Mother Earth: Native American Perspectives on Environment Justice*. New York: Orbis Books, 1996.

ACKNOWLEDGEMENTS

As a non-Native American writing this study guide, I am so appreciative of the help I have received from several Native Americans. Thanks to Thom White Wolf Fassett for an outstanding and challenging text that made my job much easier and for his support and input as I wrote this guide. Thanks to Ann Saunkeah for an extensive outline that got me started. Thanks to Dayton Edmonds and Gary Locklear for allowing me to use them as sounding boards and for their contributions to use with the study. Thanks to those Native Americans who have graciously shared resources, contacts and stories: Cynthia Kent, David Wilson, Jennifer Battiest, Anita Phillips and Harold Jacobs. And thanks to all the Native Americans who through the years shared with me and helped me to grow in my understanding of the native culture and people and to realize how much more I have to learn.

GOALS

Review the following goals and reflect on them. Consider how to present the materials in such a way as to enable the participants to have a positive outcome. If you are leading a group at a Regional or Conference School of Mission, keep in mind that upon completion of the study participants will need to be prepared to lead this study themselves. All participants should feel empowered and equipped to move into action.

- **To provide information about Native American histories, ceremonies, world views, religions and spiritualities through the lens of "Give Away."**
- **To examine these key issues and their impact:**
  - **Land**
  - **Sovereignty**
  - **Treaties**
  - **Natural resources**
  - **Poverty**
  - **Women, children and youth**
  - **Racism**
- **To explore the root causes of these issues through applying a methodological grid of race, class, culture, gender and misconceptions (e.g. media, myths of the dominant culture).**

- **To address the issue of commodification as it relates to spirituality, culture, symbols, and artifacts.**
- **To explore the impact of past Christian mission.**
- **To lift up current mission:**
  - **Exploring initiatives of the Native American Comprehensive Plan and their impact on church and society.**
  - **Considering how to influence U.S. public policies for the well-being of Native Americans.**
  - **Developing action plans and advocacy efforts as individuals to work in solidarity with Native Americans.**

PREPARING FOR THE STUDY

Essential Resources

In addition to the study book and study guide, the following are essential resources for this study:

- *New World Outlook* magazine (July/August 2007) and *Response* magazine April 2008.
- *Stories from the Circle of Life* Native American video/DVD
- *The United Methodist Hymnal* (Board of Discipleship)

Additional Resources

These resources will enhance the effectiveness of your study:

- *Voices, Native American Hymns and Worship* (Board of Discipleship, 1992)
- *Singing the Sacred: Musical Gifts from Native American Communities* (General Board of Global Ministries, available spring, 2008)
- *Native American Heritage Map*. National Geographic; 1991
  One of the finest maps of Native America ever produced. Indicates tribal and archaeological sites across the United States and southern Canada. Includes reservations and museums. Available on ebay. Or order the 2004 *North American Indian Reference Map* (item # 20315c, $12.95) at www.nationalgeographic.com.

- Prints and cards of Native American drawings and paintings as well as a CD and cassettes by Dayton Edmonds, Caddo, storyteller (Dayton Edmonds, P.O. Box 3226, Omak, WA 98841 509/826-5549). Available for purchase at HYPERLINK "http://www.daytonedmonds.net" www.daytonedmonds.net
- Three storybooks by Ray Buckley, available from Cokesbury (Cokesbury.com or 800/672-1789)

The Give-Away. Written and Illustrated by Ray Buckley. Nashville: Abingdon Press, 1999. This is more than a Christmas story. Within the message of *The Give-Away* are the themes of the Incarnation, the Atonement, stewardship, self-sacrifice, grace, giving, intercession, humility, and love. The lessons of *The Give-Away* are lessons that one grows into, understanding aspects of the work of God as experience and faith grow.

The Wing. Written and Illustrated by Ray Buckley. Nashville: Abingdon Press, 2002. Within the message of *The Wing* are the themes of healing, the importance of names within the spiritual journey, change, growth, overcoming fear, and community dynamics. *The Wing* is a story of spiritual healing. It is marginally an observation of relationships within the community, but more importantly recognition that God does not always change our circumstances, but always touches our spirit.

Christmas Moccasins. Written and Illustrated by Ray Buckley. Nashville: Abingdon Press, 2003. In this true story, a grandmother and her grandson experience being beaten and robbed by three young men. While this story takes place in the late fall and at Christmas, it is not so much a Christmas story, but a story of forgiveness and giving-away. It is a life-lesson on overcoming hurt and creating something beautiful as a way of prayer and forgiveness.

These storybooks accompany both the children's and the youth study and can provide a way to engage learners in intergenerational settings. Although in the traditional picture book format, they are written for persons of all ages. While younger children will enjoy the art and story at a simple level appropriate to their stage of development, the themes and metaphors employed are complex and multidimensional. Adults can explore and reflect at a deeper level that will be enhanced by the illustrations that accompany the text.

Other Resources and People

Tonya Gonella Frishner, President

American Indian Law Alliance

611 Broadway, Suite 632

New York, N.Y. 10012

Tel: (1-212) 477-9100

E-mail: aila@ailanyc.org

Note: The Alliance is in the process of moving. Check their website for more information.

Ali El-Issa, President

The Ingrid Washinawatok El-Issa

Flying Eagle Woman for Peace, Justice and Sovereignty

11 Broadway - 2nd Floor

New York, N.Y. 10004

Tel: (1-212) 982-5358

E-mail: ali@flyingeaglewomanfund.orag

www.flyingeaglewomanfund.org (http://www.flyingeaglewomanfund.org/)

The American Indian Community House

708 Broadway, 8th Floor

New York, N.Y. 10003

Website: National Coalition Against Domestic Violence. Go to the site to find statistics on domestic violence for each state.

Things to Consider

- Building community with the class is important as you begin. There will be participants from a variety of backgrounds and experiences, particularly if you teach in a School of Christian Mission. You will need to establish trust and to encourage an openness to different points of view.
- A variety of teaching methods is used throughout this guide. Several activities are designed for

small groups. For this study, participants form into groups as they choose based on personal interests. This means participants will probably be working with several different group members throughout the study.

- Session 1 opens with the Traditional Iroquois Prayer from the study book in responsive reading form. The other sessions use adapted and condensed sections of the prayer as a beginning meditation each day.
- There are several vignettes designed to help in understanding that this study is not just about a group of people we call Native Americans, or even Cherokee, Lakota, or Caddo. It is about families, friends, and individuals. When we connect names and individual stories with historical realities and concepts, learning often becomes more real and identifiable.

Tips for Teaching

1. **Consider your role.** It is important to remember yourself and to emphasize with your group that you are the study leader, not the teacher, and that you will all be learning from one another. The function of this guide is to assist you in facilitating the group as they explore issues and gain understanding and insight into the strong spirituality of the Native Americans and into how history has affected them as a spiritual and trusting people.
2. **Create two outlines:**
   - **Create one detailed outline** with anticipated lengths of time for each section. This is *your outline*. Be prepared with an optional learning activity in the event that something takes less time than allotted, or if a suggested activity really doesn't work with your group. Don't be afraid to delete an activity if an activity or discussion is taking longer because of the interest and involvement of the group.
   - **The second is a condensed outline for *group participants*.** Do not include times, for if you are running late with an activity, participants tend to get hung up on time rather than focusing on content.
3. **Be flexible and open to adjusting your lesson plans** as needed to meet interests and needs of the group.
4. **Find ways to encourage interaction between participants**, not just conversation between leader and participants. For example, when study participants are making a presentation to the class, they oftentimes tend to talk to the study leader. It may help if you sit near the back

of the room (and in the middle if possible) when presentations are being made.

5. **Encourage additional reading.** Recommend that those who participate in the reading program of United Methodist Women check the UMW reading list for books related to this study.
6. **Make assignments for the study at the end of the first session.** If the study is to be done in a one-day setting, try to assign specific presentations in advance to those you know will be attending the study.

PREPARE THE LEARNING SPACE

- **Place posters and pictures around the room** to create an appropriate environment for learning. Make space across a wall or on a bulletin board for displaying the timeline for the study, making sure it is positioned high enough to be easily seen but not too high for people to be able to make additions to it.
- **Display the map from the July/August 2007 *New World Outlook*** magazine that shows all the United Methodist Native American fellowships and ministries across the United States. Also try to obtain the Native American Heritage Map from National Geographic if possible.
- **The building of the triptych is suggested in the introduction to Session 1.** This is a three-sided display board constructed by joining three sheets of poster-board or foamcore board with "hinges" of tape. Three-sided display boards sold in craft stores will also work. Plan to display it on a table. For each session, attach to one of the three panels pictures, statistics, quotations and scriptures that relate to the information being presented. For the first session, fold the triptych so the remaining two sides are not readily visible. For the second and third sessions, fold the triptych to display materials related to those sessions. For the fourth session, you can open the display up completely so all three panels are visible. Or you can use a four-panel display, turning each day to display the relevant material, pictures and drawings. Another option is to use a large cardboard carton, turning the box to display the appropriate session's materials.
- **Create a worship or meditation center** reflective of the study and add to or change it daily to reflect the session focus and issues. Obtain prints of Native American drawings and paintings and change them daily.

  Dayton Edmonds, Caddo, has granted permission for study leaders to enlarge the notecards available for purchase from the website listed above (additional resources). These can be used as posters Other good resources for photos are the issues of *New World Outlook* and *Response* magazines. Buy two copies of each – one for photos and one for articles.

- **Set up a table for browsing** that includes a variety of resources. Mark each resource clearly so that participants can distinguish them from free handouts. Do not place free handouts on the same table. They can easily be mixed up.
- **Arrange seating** in such a way that everyone can see and hear everyone else. Check the session plans to see when chairs in a semi-circle may be most appropriate and when you will need tables or in chairs for small groups. In Schools of Christian Mission, learning spaces may be less flexible, with fixed theater-style seating. Be prepared to adapt to such spaces by bringing sturdy cardboard for lapboards or to place across seats for display space.

SUGGESTED OUTLINES FOR ONE, TWO OR FOUR HOUR STUDIES

One-Hour Study

- Use guided meditation from Session 1.
- View Native American Study DVD (Sections 2 & 3) and use discussion questions in the video guide.
- Look at the map from 2007 July/August *New World Outlook* magazine and locate all UM Native American Fellowships and Ministries.
- Read and discuss the vignette "Jennifer Battiest."

Two-Hour Study

- Use the guided meditation from Session 1.
- View the Native American Study DVD and use discussion questions.
- Give the Native American Quiz (Appendix C, p. 181) and discuss answers.
- Depending on the size of your group, select one or more of the four resolutions listed at the end of Session 3. Make copies of the resolution and discuss.
- Read and discuss the vignette "Jennifer Battiest."

Four-Hour Study

From Session 1:

- Use guided meditation.

- View sections from study DVD and discuss questions.
- Discuss spirituality and Native Values and engage in Biblical reflections.

From Session 2:

- Finish viewing study DVD and discuss questions.
- Discuss readings from text in small groups.
- Hold the Tribal Council simulation.
- Read and discuss vignette "Willie and Helen Senungetuk."
- Take the quiz.
- Look at the map from 2007 July/August *New World Outlook* magazine and locate all UM Native American Fellowships and Ministries.

From Session 3:

- Discuss one or more of the four resolutions in small groups. Report back to total group.
- Read and discuss the vignette "Jennifer Battiest."
- Use the benediction: "We Are God's Essence" (Session 4).

ADVANCE PREPARATION FOR PARTICIPANTS

In preparation for the study, ask class participants to research the following:

- Are there Indian reservations in your area?
- Are there tribes of Native Americans in your area but not on reservations? If so, which tribes?
- What Native American ministries are happening in your conference or jurisdiction (one resource for identifying these is July/August 2007 issue of *New World Outlook*)?
- Does your conference have an active Committee on Native American Ministries as mandated by General Conference?

SESSION 1

Introduction, Chapters 1 and 2

SCRIPTURE

JOHN 1:1-5

MATERIALS AND SUPPLIES:

- *Voices: Native American Hymns and Worship Resources*
- *Singing the Sacred: Musical Gifts from Native American Communities*
- *The United Methodist Hymnal*
- *The Give-Away* by Ray Buckley (Abingdon Press)
- photos from magazines and prints related to Native Americans and to this study (see p. 137 for sources)
- 4x6 index cards
- black felt-tipped markers
- newsprint and tape
- copies of participants' outline
- DVD *Stories from the Circle of Life* (companion for the study)
- DVD player/projector and TV
- Bibles
- tape or clothesline with clothes pins for hanging time line in order
- *(optional)* recorded Native American music and or stories

PREPARATION:

- Obtain copies of *The United Methodist Hymnal, `Voices: Native American Hymns Worship Resources, and Singing the Sacred: Musical Gifts from Native American Communities*
- If possible, obtain a copy of the storybook *The Give-Away* by Ray Buckley.
- Look over the suggested hymns and choose one for the group to sing.
- Set up the worship/meditation center with the following: baskets, decorative bowl of water, plants, strawberries, squash, corn, copy of the picture *New Home* (by Dayton Edmonds), woven cloth, Bible.

- Print the goals of the study on newsprint and display where it can be easily seen. Make copies of the participants' outline you prepared.
- Print dates for time line (Appendix A, p. 00) on 4x6 cards (or cut 8 1/2x11 paper in half). Choose a bulletin board or a section of wall where participants can construct the timeline. Or suspend a clothesline across a wall and have available paper clips or clothespins for hanging cards.
- On a table near the door, place pictures from magazines depicting issues addressed in this study. (*Response* and *New World Outlook* are good sources for the pictures.) Also have 4x6 index cards and cards, and felt-tipped markers available.
- On newsprint, print the directions for the opening activity and post above the table. Arrange chairs in groups of four.
- In a prominent place, display the triptych of pictures and quotes (see p. 140 for directions for constructing).
- Set up the DVD player and television. Check the DVD menu to see how to cue it to the beginning.

OPENING (20 MINUTES)

1. Communicate about Native Americans.

When participants come into the learning space, direct their attention to the table and the posted directions. They are to select a picture or write a word or phrase on a card in large letters that communicates something to them about Native Americans.

2. Use a Guided Meditation.

Invite everyone turn to the Traditional Iroquois Prayer Litany (Appendix B, p. 175). Divide the group into two groups (left and right side of the room) for the reading. Begin with this introduction:

Native Americans, as a people of faith, begin their meetings with a prayer or meditative reflection. As we commence our study, why should we do less as we prepare ourselves to consider religious perspectives, understandings of the movement of the Creator of people, history and time and our role in the realm of God? The following traditional opening prayer is recited by Six Nations spiritual leaders at the beginning of all meetings of the people. It is a recognition of the role of the Creator in the lives and health of the people.

Listen to the words…Listen to the sounds…Listen to the heart of the cadence…and imagine it to be the center of spiritual focus for this study.

Read the litany together.

3. Read Scripture.

Read aloud, or invite a volunteer to read, John 1:1-5.

4. Reflect.

Read *The Give-Away* by Ray Buckley. Or say the following:

God is the source of every element of life and supplies all of the helpers that sustain and nourish all of us. I call this scriptural declaration "God's giveaway." This phrase gives credence to the concept of "giveaway" or "Potlatch," practiced by most Indian nations and Native cultures. There is generally a widespread understanding that we own nothing. This applies to the land and all that God has made. Therefore, we give away those things that are needed by others as God or the Great Spirit gives to us all that we need. We share with others the Creator's bountiful gifts to us. Even when we have little, we share what we have with others who have needs.

5. Sing a Hymn.

Sing together "Kiowa Prayer Song" (*Voices: Native American Hymns and Worship*, #43), or "Many and Great, O God" (*The United Methodist Hymnal*, #148 – Native American melody).

6. Get Acquainted.

Ask participants to introduce themselves by telling their name, where they are from and in *two or three sentences only*, why they selected the picture or wrote the word or phrase they did. If you like, invite participants to tape their cards or pictures to a large sheet of newsprint to make a collage.

LEARNING ACTIVITIES (60 MINUTES)

7. Introduce the Study.

Hand out the participants' outline and introduce the study to the class. Call attention to the study goals you prepared and posted. Give a brief overview using the Introduction of the text and then quickly walk the class through the chapters, calling attention to headings as well as to the scope of the text.

8. Show the DVD.

Show the opening of the study video (2 minutes) and Part 1: "The Spiritual Lessons and Tradition of Faith" (9 minutes). Then discuss spirituality and native values. **ASK:**

- **When we talk about Native spirituality and values, what are the elements that come to mind?**

Draw a vertical line down the center of a sheet of newsprint or on a chalkboard or whiteboard and list these on the right side of center line. Leave space to the left for writing Bible verses that correlate to each item.

Be sure the following values are included:

- Respect for creation
- Worship and prayer
- Humility (compassion, truth, sacrifice, love)
- Sense of community
- Relationships – importance of extended family
- Importance of elders
- Give-away
- Oral tradition and preservation of language/traditions

BREAK (5 MINUTES)

9. Reflect on Scripture.

Invite participants to divide into self-selected groups of four. Ask them to compare the creation stories found in Genesis 1 and 2 with that found in *Stories from the Circle of Life*.

Also invite them to find Bible passages that correlate with the values listed prior to the break.

When groups have had several minutes to work, bring them back to the total group. In turn ask each group to call out scripture references they found for each value. Record their responses on the right side of the newsprint sheet beside Native spirituality and values. **ASK:**

- **Where do we find similarities between Native American values and spirituality and the Bible? What differences do we see?**

10. Construct a Timeline.

Continuing in the small groups, make the following reading assignments:

Group 1: Chapter 1, p. 17 to top of p. 26

Group 2: Chapter 1, pp. 26-31 (beginning with "Native Religion and Government")

Group 3: Chapter 2, p. 33 to top of p. 38

Group 4: Chapter 2, pp. 38-45 (beginning with "Beginnings of Methodism in America")

Give each group twenty minutes to read, discuss the assigned pages, and prepare a report for the total group. Ask each group to select a reporter.

Invite the respective groups to find the cards with dates that are significant for the time period on which they are reporting and to add them in sequence to the timeline.

Beginning with Group 1, allow three to four minutes per group for reporting and pointing out relevant dates the group added to the timeline (Note: Group 2 will not have any dates). **SAY:**

As we look at our history, we see how the beliefs and values of the Native people were affected with the arrival of the colonists in this country where the Indians were already inhabitants.

Ask group members to respond to the following:

- **Were there particular events that affected the spirituality and values of the Native Americans?**
- **What has been done in the name of Christianity in our relationships with Native people over the last five hundred years?**
  - **How has this affected the Native Americans?**
  - **How has it affected non-Natives?**
- **Do you see contradictions when we talk about the separation of church and state and religious freedom in regard to how Native Americans have been and are being treated?**
- **What are unfinished/unanswered questions arising out of this study?** *(list on newsprint)*

CLOSING (10 MINUTES)

11. Make Assignments.

Make the following assignments for Session 2 and 3 of the study:

- Ask for two volunteers to prepare monologues/dialogues for Session 2 on the following vignettes (pp. 189-191)
  - Chief Seattle
  - Willie and Helen Senungetuk
- Divide participants into four groups for Session 2. Again allow them to choose the group of their choice. Ask them to read the following from the text in preparation for their group:
  - Chapter 3, pp. 47-52
  - Chapter 3, pp. 53-61
  - Chapter 4, pp. 63-72
- For the skit in Session 3, ask for volunteers to take the following parts:
  - Moderator
  - Two commercial announcers
  - Jennifer Battiest
  - Betty Hodson
  - Gary Locklear
  - Fran Lynch
  - Wilma Mankiller
- Also ask for signups for the stories that will come from the audience (See Session 3).

12. Sing a Hymn.

Sing: "Orphan Child" or "One Drop of Blood," Cherokee songs from the Trail of Tears (*Singing the Sacred: Musical Gifts from Native American Communities*).

13. Pray Together.

Read "Prayer to the Holy Spirit" (*The United Methodist Hymnal*, #329).

SESSION 2

Chapters 3, 4 and 5

SCRIPTURE
PSALM 24: 1-2

MATERIALS AND SUPPLIES:

- Bibles and hymnals for each participant (*The United Methodist Hymnal, Voices, Native American Hymns and Worship* and *Singing the Sacred: Musical Gifts from Native American Communities*)
- DVD player and TV monitor
- *Stories from the Circle of Life*, DVD for this study
- Copies of information from website and cards for simulation (see Preparation)
- Newsprint, tape and felt-tipped markers
- Newsprint with small group tasks (see Preparation)
- Copies of quiz for participants (Appendix C, P. 181)
- Materials for meditation/worship center (see Preparation)

PREPARATION:

- Get copies of either the *United Methodist Hymnal* or *Voices, Native American Hymns and Worship*. Go over the phonetic pronunciations of the words to "Amazing Grace."
- Set up the DVD player and TV monitor. Cue the DVD at Part 2.
- Go to the website HYPERLINK "http://www.mapcruzin.com/ejigc.html" www.mapcruzin.com/ejigc.html. Download and print the information there to use in the simulation activity (Activity # 6). Also prepare the following cards:
  - 2 cards that reads "strongly support the contract"
  - 1 card that reads "supports because of millions which will come to the tribe"
  - 2 cards that read "strongly oppose the contract"

– 1 card that reads "oppose because loss of sacred land and cost to yet unborn tribal members"

– 2 cards that read "will present the contract for toxic waste dump on tribal land – millions of dollars"

– 2or 3 cards that read "hope to have gatekeeper responsibilities for benefits coming to tribe"

– remaining cards that read "undecided – take position you wish"

- Make copies of the quiz for all class participants (Appendix D, p. 185). Plan to hand out copies at the end of class period.
- Obtain newsprint, tape and felt-tipped markers.
- Add candles, a bowl and a pitcher of water to the meditation center. Print the names of treaties on sheets of paper in large letters. Then tear the sheets in half (symbolizing broken treaties) and place in the center. Remove the picture for Session 1 and add *A Common Peace* (or one of your choice).
- Set up the space to accommodate three groups, with three tables if possible. On each table place one of the following placards or signs:

  – Native Women and Families (pp. 47-52)

  – Treaties and Schooling (pp. 53-61)

  – Great American Take-Away (pp. 63-72)
- On newsprint, print the following tasks for the small group discussion:

  – Where appropriate, add information to the time line.

  – Identify key issues.

  – How do these actions correlate with the spirituality and Native values?

  – What new information did you learn from this reading?
- Also set up chairs in a semicircle around the meditation/worship center.

OPENING (10 MINUTES)

1. Read a Responsive Reading.

Invite participants to come together for opening worship. Read the following together:

Leader: As we prepare for the day, let us gather in this meeting place to remember what the

Creator has done…

Let us thank our Creator for each other.

All: **Let us put our minds together as one mind and greet each other.**

(Allow time for greetings.)

Leader: Look out and see the earth and all it provides to support our life. We see all these good things coming from the earth and we give thanks. *(Pour water from pitcher into bowl.)*

Let us be reminded of many kinds of waters – from mountain streams, rivers lakes and salt waters. We are dependent on these waters for our life and well-being.

All: **Let us put our minds together as one mind and give thanksgiving.**

Leader: As we look about, we see many growing things – plants, berries and all kinds of food. We see trees that provide food and shelter.

All: **For all these we give thanksgiving.**

Leader: We see the animal life that provides us food to eat and clothing to wear. As we look to the sky, we see those of the bird kingdom that gives us song and tell us of warm winds blowing.

All: **For all these we give thanksgiving.**

Leader: We look above and see the skies – the sun – the moon – the stars – that lead and guide us. There are the ones who are responsible for bringing us the good news telling us how to go about and carry on in this world and to carry ourselves in this creation.

All: **We put our minds together as one mind and extend a greeting and a thanksgiving.**

Leader: And now there is the Creator, the great mystery. It is the Creator that brought us all of these things and asks us to be thankful and grateful to all that we see about us for they are the ones who give us life.

All: **And so as we gather here we put our minds together as one mind and extend a greeting and thanksgiving to our Creator.**

2. Read Scripture.

Read aloud, or ask a volunteer to read, Psalm 24: 1-2.

3. Hear a Vignette.

Ask the participant who volunteered at the end of Session 1 to present the monologue of the vignette by Chief Seattle.

4. Sing a Hymn.

Invite participants to practice saying the phonetic transcriptions to some or all of the following to "Amazing Grace": Cherokee, Navajo, Kiowa, Creek or Choctaw. Then sing "Amazing Grace" (*Voices* #6 or *The United Methodist Hymnal* #378).

LEARNING ACTIVITIES (70 MINUTES)

5. View the Video/DVD.

View Part 2 of the video/DVD: "Cries of Justice, Saving Our Earth" (12 minutes).

Discuss, using the following questions:

- **What are some of the prophetic lessons and messages we learn from the history? What are the lessons of the elders?**
- **How will the actions affect all God's children?**
- **How is the Native American experience integrated into the life of the church?**
- **What are the challenges today as the Native Americans live out their faith in society and within the church?**
- **In the text, Thom White Wolf Fassett comments that the American Indian is the miner's canary. In the past Native American children were taken from their families and cultures and imprisoned in schools many miles – oftentimes states away – from their parents. They were bombarded with the message that their traditional ways of life were savage and inhumane. Drugs were first tested on Native peoples. What are the poisonous effects of such history?**
- **What stereotypes are used to label our Native brothers and sister year after year?**

6. Discuss in Small Groups.

Invite participants to go to the table with the small group they chose last session. Ask each group to choose a leader to facilitate the discussion and a reporter to print on newsprint the key points of the discussion. The reporter will then share with the total group, each taking no more than four minutes. Call the group's attention to the tasks and questions you printed on newsprint. Ask them to use the tasks to guide their discussion.

BREAK (5 MINUTES)

During break, ask those participants who prepared reports on work being done by the church with Native Americans in their conference or area to sign up with the name of the project, town and state. Be prepared to make assignments at the end of the session. Also rearrange the room, setting up chairs theater style. Set up a table and three chairs at the front of the space.

7. Hold a Tribal Council Meeting Simulation.

Say the following:

Today, you, as the Tribal Council, will be electing a chair, vice chair and secretary. Do we have nominations for a chair?

Take the nominations and write them on the board. When nominations are completed, take the vote to elect the Tribal Council chair. Turn the nominating and election process of the vice chair and secretary over to the chair. After the officers have been elected, pass out the cards you prepared to the remaining participants who will be the Tribal Council.

SAY:

The tribal council government acknowledges the federal authority. It is this same body that enters into all federal contracts on behalf of the tribe. It acts as the gate keeper for all benefits the tribes derive from being under the tutelage of the Bureau of Indian Affairs. You, the tribal council, will hear a proposal for a contract to use some of your tribal land for toxic waste dumping. There are two people here who will bring this proposal, which will bring several million dollars to the tribe. After hearing the proposal, you will debate the issue and vote.

SAY to the chair:

You have fifteen minutes to hear the proposal and debate the issue. You can include in the debate moral and ethical standards that are part of the traditions of the Indian nation. You will then need to deal with any other business related to this proposal, as we must vacate the room after that.

At this point, turn the "meeting" over to the chair and let the council begin.

After the simulated debate, discuss the following:

1. **What were the issues presented to support the various sides?**
2. **Were the positions and issues presented equally and fairly?**
3. **How did you feel about the position to which you were assigned?**
4. **How did you feel about the outcome?**
5. **Other comments?**

8. Take a Quiz.

Hand out copies of the quiz. Ask participants to take the quiz, realizing that some of the questions have not been covered in the reading. Say that In the last session, the group will go over the quiz and discuss the answers, so everyone needs to make sure they bring the completed quiz to the last session.

CLOSING (10 MINUTES)

9. Make Assignments.

Check the sign up sheet to look for any overlaps with more than one participant having the same project. Ask those with the same project to work together on sharing their information. Designate four to six participants to share with the class in Session 3 about the ministry they have researched and what is happening in their area or conference. Say that you will limit the time to two minutes per report. If you are teaching in a School of Mission, try to choose participants from several areas to report.

If you do not have enough people with information to share or if all have basically the same one or two projects, select additional stories from the April 2007 issue of *Response* magazine. In the July/August 2006 issue of *New World Outlook.* consider sharing the following stories: "The Oklahoma Indian Missionary Conference Disaster Response Team" by David Wilson, "Four Corners Native American Ministry" by Roger Tsosie, "The Navajo Nation Welcomes the Church" by Paul West. The July/August 2007 issue of *New World Outlook* contains excellent stories as well.

Ask for volunteers to be readers for the meditation in the next session.

10. Sing a Hymn.

Sing "Okou Aloaha No (The Queen's Prayer)" (*Singing the Sacred: Musical Gifts from Native American Communities*).

11. Hear a Vignette.

Ask a volunteer to read aloud "Sand Creek Massacre" (Appendix F, p.198).

Close with the following statement by Chief Joseph Nez Perce:

We were told to treat all people as they treated us;
That we should never be the first to break a bargain;
That it was a disgrace to tell a lie; that we should
Speak only the truth; that it was a shame for one man
To take from another without paying for it.

SESSION 3

Chapters 6 and 7

SCRIPTURE

PSALM 8

MATERIALS AND SUPPLIES:

- Bibles and hymnals
- DVD player and TV monitor
- *Stories from the Circle of Life* DVD
- tables for small group work
- signs to identify groups
- "Agree" and "disagree" signs (see Preparation)
- Newsprint, tape and felt-tipped markers
- Newsprint with questions for Activity #8 (see Preparation)
- (optional) *The Christmas Moccasins* by Ray Buckley

PREPARATION:

- Add branches of maple leaves to the meditation/worship center. Also place the picture *No More Tears* or one of your own choice in the center.
- Set up the space to accommodate six groups, with tables if possible. Place a sign in the center of each table identifying the topic with which each group will be dealing.
- Cue the DVD to play Part 3.
- Decide which musical prayer the group will sing (see Activity #3).
- Put up two signs on opposite sides of the room — "Agree" and "Disagree."
- Obtain newsprint, tape and felt-tipped markers.
- On newsprint, print the following questions for Activity #8:

  1. What are the issues and what is currently happening or not happening?
  2. What are the resources?

3. How are we going to respond? Include timeline, resources needed; information, people and money.

Post where it can be easily seen.

- (optional) Get a copy of *The Christmas Moccasins* by Ray Buckley.

OPENING (10 MINUTES)

1. Read a Responsive Reading.

Read the following together:

Leader: We are gathered in this meeting place to tell what the Creator has done.

All: **As we look about us we see people who have come together for the purpose of study, understanding and growth, so we put our minds together as one mind and greet one another.**

Reader 1: We look about us and see the one we call our mother the earth. She is the supporter of all of life and we see that all of these good things are coming to us from the earth.

Reader 2: As we look about, we see that there is all of the tree life living abundantly on this land. It is the trees that we use for our houses. Some of the trees provide us with fruits and others provide flowers that brighten our spirits. There is a special tree on the earth; this is the maple tree. This is the first to awaken from the sleep of winter and its sweet sap will be used in ceremonies.

All: **And so to all good things coming from mother earth and the tree life growing on the land, we put our minds together as one mind and extend a greeting and thanksgiving.**

Reader 3: Again, as we look about us we see those who are always watching us—the ones we call our grandfathers, the four winds. The four winds bring us the rains and will keep the air clean for us. They have carried on in the most ancient ways as the Creator has told them carrying with the clouds and the thunders that will give us water to drink.

Reader 4: We see the one we call our elder brother the sun, the daytime light. He is still bringing warmth and light upon the land so that we go about on the earth and do not bump into one another and cause conflicts and troubles.

Reader 5: As we look into the sky, we see there is another, the one we call the night time light, our grandmother moon. The moon will always follow the path across the sky as she fulfills the original instructions. We also know that it is grandmother who is the leader of all female life.

All: **Let us put our minds together as one mind and extend a greeting and thanksgiving to our grandfathers the four winds, our elder brother the sun, and for grandmother moon.**

Reader 6: There is the Creator, the great mystery. It is the Creator that brought us all these things and we know that all that is necessary for life and happiness is provided for us.

All: **And so as we gather here we put our minds together as one mind and extend a greeting and thanksgiving to our Creator.**

2. Hear a Vignette.

Invite the volunteers who prepared a dialogue on the vignette "Willie and Helen Senungetuk" to present it for the group.

3. Read Scripture.

Read aloud, or invite a volunteer to read, Psalm 8.

4. Pray with Music.

Sing together "All Things Hold Beauty" (*Voices, Native American Hymns and Worship*, # 69) or "Scripture with Choral Response, Psalm 8") – choral response 2, "Many and Great, O God" (*The United Methodist Hymnal*, #743).

LEARNING ACTIVITIES (75 MINUTES)

5. Reflect on the Reading.

ASK:

- **In reading for today, what was new information for you?**
- **What dates do we need to lift up on our timeline?**

Discuss any questions that may have surfaced for the group as they read. Make note of areas where more information may be needed.

6. Place Yourself on a Continuum.

Point out for the group the two signs reading "Agree" and "Disagree" that you posted on opposite sides of the room. Say that you will read a statement. They are to consider whether they agree or disagree with the statement, and to what degree, and to place themselves along the continuum at a place that reflects their position on the statement. Participants can stand directly next to one sign or the other or anywhere in between those two points. After reading each statement, ask participants to respond as to why they took the stand they did. Use the following statements (to which you may add others):

1. Many of the Native American traditions affirm the presence of God, the need for right relationship with our Creator, the world around us, and a call for holy living.
2. There is controversy surrounding the fact that Native American tribes own casinos and sponsor other forms of gaming on the reservations. I think gaming should be supported because of the additional revenues it will generate for the Native Americans.
3. While it is appalling that the lands are being mutilated by oil and coal companies, in this time of energy scarcity and high fuel costs, this needs to be allowed.

7. View the DVD.

View Part 3 of the DVD, "Can Reconciliation Occur?" (5 min.).

Discuss the following questions:

- After hundreds of years of broken treaties and agreements and violated trust, can non-Indians and Native Americans be God's family together?
- When one population has abused another population, can healing and reconciliation occur without feelings of paternalism?
- Can the majority population learn humility and lessons from a minority population?

BREAK (5 MINUTES)

8. Prepare to Respond.

SAY:

Through this mission study on Native Americans, we have examined what has happened over the centuries and learned where we are today. However, if we leave here saying,

"That was a good study. Isn't it awful how the Native Americans have been treated? Something needs to be done," and that is the end, the study has failed. As United Methodists, we are called to action.

Divide participants into small groups of three to six people each to work on ways to respond, either individually or collectively. The first four suggested responses are from the *2004 Book of Resolutions* (Appendix C, p. 181). Invite the group to identify at least two other options that have arisen as issues in discussions. Say that they will have the remainder of the time until the closing worship in this session to work in the small groups and that they should plan to report back to the total group in Session 4

- 130 – "Concerning Demeaning Names to Native Americans"
- 134 – "Health Care for Native Americans"
- 137 – "Native American Ministries Sunday"
- 143 – "Native American Religious Freedom Act"
- ______________________________
- ______________________________

If group members are interested, say that they might also form groups around other concerns, such as the Committee on Native American Ministries in your area (find out what they are doing. If there is not one, they could contact the Bishop's office about organizing one); the Native American Comprehensive Plan, or sponsoring Native American scholarships to attend national events.

Call their attention to the posted questions that will help to shape their report and invite them to list their responses on newsprint.

Alert those who volunteered to be a part of the skit next session, asking that they remain for a few minutes after the session to run through the script (Appendix D, p. 185) Also remind participants who signed up to make reports on projects in their area in the next session. The reports will be a part of the skit.

CLOSING (5 MINUTES)

9. Close with a Reading.

Read the storybook *The Christmas Moccasins* by Ray Buckley or read "We Pray Your Wisdom" (*Voices*).

SESSION 4

Chapter 8 and Last Word

SCRIPTURE

LUKE 4:18 -19

MATERIALS AND SUPPLIES:

- Bibles and hymnals
- Items for the meditation/worship center (see Preparation)
- Signs for the skit (see Preparation)
- *Stories from the Circle of Life* DVD
- DVD player and TV monitor

PREPARATION:

- Add the following to the meditation/worship center: pitcher of water, bowl, towel, bundle of five sticks and individual sticks. Change the picture to *Music Makers* or one of your choice.
- Set up the chairs theater style for the skit. Also set up five chairs in the center across the front for the guests and "Host Sarah" and two chairs to one side. Over the two chairs, post a sign that reads, "Commercial Spotlight."
- In large black letters, print name cards for those to be interviewed in the skit: Jennifer Battiest, Betty Hodgson, Gary Locklear, Fran Lynch, Wilma Mankiller.
- Set up the DVD player and TV monitor.

OPENING (10 MINUTES)

1. Sing a Hymn.

Sing "Jesus, Our Friend and Brother." (*The United Methodist Hymnal*, #659).

2. Read a Responsive Reading.

Read the following together:

Leader: We are gathered in this meeting place to tell what the Creator has done.

All: **As it is our custom when we are gathered, we are to indicate a high regard for one another. We see that all of the people are healthy and happy and there have been few or no disasters, no or, at least, little illness.**

Leader: As we look about us we see that the first thing people do when they come together is that they greet one another before going about their business…

All: **And so we put our minds together as one mind and greet one another.**

(Time to greet each other)

Leader: There are the ones responsible for bringing us the good news telling us how to go about and carry on in this world.

All: **It is these who have tried to help us understand where we are and to carry ourselves in this creation.**

Leader: And now there is the Creator, the great mystery.

All: **It is the Creator that brought us all of these things and we know that all that is necessary for life and happiness is provided for us.**

Leader: And it is true, that no one will know the Creator's face as we travel about on this earth but…

All: **That the Creator simply asks one another be thankful and grateful to all that we see about us for they are the ones who give us life.**

Leader: And now, if there is anything that has been left out and the people listening have remembered a special thing that should receive a greeting and a thanksgiving, it should be remembered that we have not learned all to which we are to give greetings; other times we are forgetful. If there are things that have been left out, now is the time to extend a special greeting and thanksgiving.

(Invite participants to share joys and concerns).

4. Read Scripture.

Read aloud, or invite a volunteer to read, Luke 4:18 -19.

5. Hear a Meditation.

Invite someone from the group to break one of the single sticks, symbolic of an arrow, in half. Next, hand them the bundle of sticks tied together and ask them to break the bundle in half.

SAY:

A single stick is easily broken. However, the bundle of identical sticks could not be successfully broken in half. So it is that in isolation we do not have the strength that we have together. Among Native people, community is both a place and a value. Community is also the way in which one lives. Most reservation children know what it is like to have "one hundred mothers." Community is caring for one another. It is sharing all that you have, but it is also an awareness that others will share with you. It is being part of something larger than you. Native tribes, communities, customs and languages have been fought for and maintained at great price. Community for Native people means not only roots, but also branches reaching far and deep into our lives.

– Nations of the Iroquois Confederacy illustration adapted from *Walking in These White Man Shoes: Youth Explore Native America* by Ray Buckley

6. Sing a Hymn.

Sing "Heleluyan" (*The United Methodist Hymnal*, # 78).

LEARNING ACTIVITIES (65 MINUTES)

7. Answer the Quiz.

Invite participants to take out the completed Quiz on Native Americans (have available some extra copies in case someone forgot). Ask for responses from participants, adding background information from Appendix B. After you have gone through the questions, ask participants to respond with what was new information for them and any other comments they may have.

8. Present a Skit.

Invite participants to present the skit, "On the Air with NAUM: Native Americans and the United Methodist Church Today" (Appendix D). Those who do not have a speaking part will make up the audience for the "show."

9. Share Resources and Techniques.

If this is a study at a Regional or Conference School of Mission, take a few minutes to discuss additional resources participants might use in their own studies, or alternate teaching techniques that might be used in place of various activities.

BREAK (5 MINUTES)

10. Report on Responding.

Invite each of the groups who worked on an action response in Session 3 to report. Remind them to use the questions to which they responded as the framework for their report, and to take no more than five minutes.

11. View the DVD.

View Part 4 and the conclusion of the DVD.

CLOSING (10 MINUTES)

12. Read Scripture.

Read aloud, or ask a volunteer to read, Psalm 133.

13. Sing a Hymn.

Sing "The Goodness of God" (*Singing the Sacred: Musical Gifts from Native American Communities*).

14. Participate in The Water Ceremony.

Invite participants who are able to stand for the Water Ceremony, a Caddo tradition that is normally done outside early in the morning where there is a body of water. But The Water Ceremony can also be done inside as a part of worship, pouring water from a pitcher into a basin to represent the movement of a stream. Say that you will read through the Water Ceremony, pausing to allow time for reflection and prayers. Then each person will experiences having water poured from the vessel onto the hands, and will wipe his or her face with water. Invite everyone to face east as you begin to read.

SAY:

The Water Ceremony from the Caddo tradition is normally done early in the morning. Facing east, the person steps into the water and then immerses the body up to the neck four times. The immersions represent the four directions; the four phases of the moon; the four seasons; and the four phases of human life (infancy, youth, adult and elder). After the fourth immersion the person splashes a handful of water on the face.

Remaining in the water, the person offers a morning prayer: giving thanks and gratitude for the new day. Let's offer our own silent prayers *(pause for a few moments)*. **Let's now pray for constant awareness** *(pause for a few moments)*. **Now let's ask for direction on how to be helpful to the creation today** *(pause for a few moments)*. **This is a time for remembrance. One is in touch with water from which creation began, in touch with the waters that surrounded life in the mother's womb, in touch with one's baptismal waters, in touch with the Mystery** *(pause for a few moments)*.

Following the time of prayer and moments of quietness, the person then immerses the body in the water two more times (the fifth immersion representing the earth, and the sixth, the sky). All six immersions combined represent the one Spirit of God and become part of the great thanksgiving. "Amen" is not said during the ceremony until the end of the day because the whole day becomes a personal prayer. After leaving the water and again facing the East, each person walks into the day with prayer and life as one.

After reading the meditation, invite participants one by one to walk to the basin, where you will pour water over their hands. They then will wipe their faces with water (have towels available for participants to dry hands and faces).

(Adapted from Caddo tradition Water Ceremony by Dayton Edmonds (Caddo), retired Church and Community Worker, as printed in Voices. Used by permission).

15. Close with a Benediction.

All: **We Are God's Essence**

Leader: God is before us.

All: **God is behind us.**

Leader: God is above us,

All: **God is below us.**

Leader: God's words shall come from our mouths.

All: **For we are all God's essence, a sign of God's love.**

Leader: All is finished in beauty.

All: **All is finished in beauty.**

(From Navajo prayer tradition as printed in *Voices*. Used with permission)

APPENDICES

APPENDIX A

Walking through Native History: European Contact through Present Day

1492-2007

1492 Christopher Columbus explores Native lands in the Americas.

1492 Estimated 12.5 million Native persons live in region that will become North America. Largest population of Native people and number of distinct tribes located in the region we now call California.

1494 Columbus ships Native people to Spain to be sold as slaves (200 years of forced labor and slavery of Native people in the Southwest would follow).

1621 Native children attend school in Jamestown, Virginia.

1638 First reservation established in Connecticut for the Quinnipiacs.

1670 Indian slave trade instituted by the English in the American southeast (Indian slave trade in the southeast would continue until 1717).

1700 Indian population in California area estimated at 750,000.

1827 Constitution of the Cherokee Nation adopted.

1830 Congress affirms forced Indian removal from the southeast to Indian Territory (three Methodist Episcopal annual conferences would support the removal).

1831 The United States Supreme Court passes ruling that tribes possess "unquestionable rights" to all lands on which they live unless they give them up voluntarily.

1834 Indian Country Crimes Act.

1836 Forced removal of Creek Nation.

1836 Beginning of 34 years of smallpox epidemics among Plains tribes (smallpox-infected blankets deliberately distributed to Native people).

1838 First of forced removals of Cherokee to Indian Territory (Native Methodists bring their churches to Indian Territory).

1841 First Methodist hymnal in Creek language.

1844 First Annual Conference of the Oklahoma Indian Missionary Conference held.

1848 Indian population in California estimated at 150,000. In 1870, only 30,000 remain.

1860 The Massacre of the Wyot Tribe (California).

1863 Forced removal of Mescalero Apache and Navajo, known as the Long Walk.

1863 Emancipation Proclamation—end of Indian Slavery.

1864 Teaching Native children in their own language prohibited by Congressional action.

1868 Fort Laramie Treaty.

1870 Supreme Court ruling affirms that Indians are not U.S. citizens.

1870 Beginning of slaughter by non-Native hunters of ten million buffalo for hides alone. Continuing until 1885, this program was designed to starve and demoralize Native people.

1875 Seventy-two warriors of the Cheyenne, Kiowa, Comanche, and Caddo nations sent to Ft. Augustine, Florida in chains and held hostage to insure that their people remain "good."

1876 Gold discovered in Black Hills. Congress "takes back" the Black Hills from land given to the Lakota Sioux.

1876 Battle of the Little Big Horn.

1879 Carlisle Indian School founded in Carlisle, PA. Native children as young as four years old are sent to boarding schools run by the Bureau of Indian Affairs (BIA) or sponsored by churches. Five generations of Native children raised in institutions without their families.

1880 Sun Dance outlawed by the U.S. federal government.

1881 Beginning of a series of policies making Native religions and customs illegal.

1885 Congress passes the Major Crimes Act.

1887 The General Allotment Act (The Dawes Act) requires tribal persons to register and allots each family a portion of land. The vast majority of lands granted under treaty are then declared excess, taken from tribes and made available for general settlement.

1890 Massacre of Lakota Sioux at Wounded Knee.

1900 Only about 250,000 Native people survive in the U.S.

1906 Cherokee Nation and other Oklahoma tribes officially terminated.

1912 Jim Thorpe (Sac and Fox tribe) wins the pentathlon and decathlon at the Olympic games in Stockholm, Sweden.

1924 Native Americans are granted U.S. citizenship.

1935 Indian Reorganization (lasting until 1953).

1940 Indian men register for draft for the first time (Native men had fought in every war since the Revolution. As new citizens, their names are entered into the draft).

1944 Navajo "code talkers" develop secret codes used in the South Pacific field of World War II. Comanche, Cheyenne, and others develop different codes also used in the war. During World War I, Choctaw soldiers had developed codes to transfer information in Europe.

1946 Policy of Indian relocation to urban centers is instituted to break down reservation systems. Families are often split up.

1953 Termination of tribes by the U.S. federal government (a fifteen year period whereby the U.S. federal Government removes tribal status and reservation lands from tribes).

1958 Lumbees force Ku Klux Klan to leave Robeson County, NC.

1968 Congress passes the Indian Civil Rights Act, basically requiring tribes to grant to Native people the same rights guaranteed to most Americans by the Bill of Rights.

1971 Alaska Native Claims Settlement Act (Federal recognition of Alaska Native people. Establishment of 13 Native corporations).

1972 Cherokee Nation re-established.

1973 American Indian Movement occupation of Wounded Knee.

1978 Congress passes the American Indian Religious Freedom Act.

1978 Indian Child Welfare Act (prohibiting states and social agencies from removing and adopting Native children without consent of their parents or tribes).

1979 Florida Seminole Nation begins first Native high-stakes bingo.

1980 Kateri Tekakwitha beatified—First Native Roman Catholic saint

1988 Indian Gaming Regulatory Act.

1989 Congress passes the National Museum of the American Indian Act.

1990 The Native American Graves Protection and Repatriation Act (requiring return of Native religious artifacts and bones by museums).

1990 Congress passes the Indian Arts and Crafts Act, stipulating that only enrolled tribal members may display in Indian Arts Shows or use the term "Indian made." Many well-known, non-enrolled artists are disenfranchised.

1993 Congress passes the Religious Freedom Restoration Act.

1995 One million Native people are members of federally recognized tribes. BIA estimates that over 500,000 U.S. born, ethnic Native people are ineligible for various reasons.

2000 Jim Thorpe (1887-1953) named by Congress as Athlete of the Century.

2007 Less than 200 Native languages still surviving. As many as 50 percent of Native people in the U.S. ineligible for tribal membership.

— From *Walking in These White Man Shoes: Youth Explore Native America* by Ray Buckley

APPENDIX B

Traditional Iroquois Prayer Responsive Reading

Leader: We are gathered in this meeting place to tell what the Creator has done.

Right: As it is our custom when we are gathered, we are to indicate a high regard for one another. We see that all of the people are healthy and happy and there have been few or no disasters, no or at least little illness.

Left: As we look about us we see that the first thing people do when they come together is that they greet one another before going about their business and so we put our minds together as one mind and greet one another.

Leader: We look about us and see the one we call our mother the earth.

Right: Mother earth is the one who is carrying on in the most ancient of ways, still following the original instructions of the Creator.

Left: She is the supporter of all feet and all of life and we see that all of these good things are coming to us from the earth.

All: So let us put our minds together as one mind and extend a greeting and thanksgiving to our mother the earth.

Leader: Looking about us we see that there are many kinds of water beings on the earth.

Right: Some of them are flowing from the mountains and they speak to us with their many voices.

Left: We see also the rivers. They are sometimes deep and slow moving. Others are rushing with torrents of power.

Right: We also see the lakes and the great salt waters. As we look about we know they are strong and they lift our spirits when we see them.

Left: It is the waters we first use in the morning. They keep us clean and healthy. We also use these waters to cook.

Leader: We know that all of these lives exist in the world because of the waters. Let us put our minds together as one mind and extend a greeting and thanksgiving.

Leader: As we continue looking about the earth, we see that there are many things growing on the earth.

Right: There are plants and grasses which form a blanket or a carpet for our mother the earth.

Left: We know we have been using these things to sustain our lives.

Right: We have used these things for medicines and they have helped us at all times.

Left: As we look about we realize these plants that grow from the earth help us to pick up our spirits with fine aroma and things of good nature that make us feel proud.

Leader: We see also the berries and we see all kinds of things we use as foods.

Right: We are always using these and without them, we would not be able to carry on in this world.

Left: There is a special berry which is the leader of the berry kingdom. We call it the strawberry. It is the first plant to bear its fruit after the long and cold winter. And we use it in our ceremonies and also as a medicine.

Leader: There are the ones among us from the plant kingdom who are related to the women and we call them the three sisters – the corn, bean and squash.

Right: The corn, bean and squash should be included in ceremonies whenever the great thanksgiving is recited.

Left: They are the sustainers of our lives. They are the ones to whom we turn at all times during the year.

Leader: As we look about, we see that there is all of the tree of life living abundantly on this land.

Right: It is the trees that we use for our houses.

Left: Some of the trees provide us with fruits and others provide flowers that will brighten our spirits.

Right: There is a special tree on earth, one that we might look at as the head tree or the leading tree; this is the maple tree.

Leader: And we put our minds together as one mind and extend a greeting and thanksgiving to these plants that grow from the earth for our health.

Leader: We see that there are the four-legged ones wandering around about on the earth; our cousins, the animals, as we are told, were put here as company for us two-legged ones.

Right: They will provide us with food to eat and, sometimes, they will provide clothing for us to wear.

Left: They will provide us with knowledge about how we should go about on this earth.

Leader: And so to the four-legged animals, we put our minds together as one mind and extend a greeting and thanksgiving.

Leader: Looking towards the sky, we see that there are those with feathers, those of the bird kingdom.

Right: We know there are many kinds that return to us to tell us of the warm winds blowing and with their songs they enlighten our spirits in the spring.

Left: They bring us a good thought and sometimes they bring us good messages and we look to them and we are given good feelings as we look to them.

Right: As we look high into the sky we see one that stands out above all others.

Left: It is the eagle.

Right: It is the eagle that flies the highest, it is the eagle that flies closest to the sun, the one whose feathers we use as one who comes closest to the Creator among those moving about on the earth.

Left: And so we know that it is the birds that are helping us moving about on the earth.

Leader: Again, as we look about us, we see those who are always about us and always watching us – the ones we call our grandfathers, the four winds.

Right: It is the four winds who bring us the rains and will keep the air clean for us.

Left: We know the four directions they come from each with a certain time to be with us each year.

Right: They have carried on in the most ancient ways as the Creator has told them carrying with them the clouds and the thunders that will give us water to drink.

Left: And we know without our grandfathers, we would not be able to carry on in this world.

Leader: We see that one we call our elder brother the sun, the daytime light.

Right: We know that it is our elder brother sun that is still carrying on the most ancient ways.

Left: He is still bringing warmth and light upon the land so that as we go about on the earth we will not bump into another and cause conflicts and troubles.

Leader: As we look into the sky, we see there is another, the one we call the nighttime light, our grandmother, the moon.

Right: The moon will always follow the path across the sky as she fulfills the original instructions.

Left: It is she who is looking over all water life and every day, the waters will rise and fall according to the ancient ways.

Right: Whenever the plants grow they are growing by her power.

Left: We also know that it is grandmother moon who is the leader of all female life.

Right: She is the one who determines birth and every month she will renew her cycles, the cycles of the female life in this world.

Leader: And so we want to put our minds together as one mind and extend a greeting and thanksgiving to our grandfathers the four winds; our elder brother the sun; and our grandmother the moon.

And so we look even higher into the sky. We see the stars and the starlight and we know that it is the stars that give the morning dew.

Right: We know that it is the starlight that has provided direction to us so that we will not get lost.

Left: The stars will help us to know when to plant and when to have our ceremonies.

Leader: And so too, there are the ones responsible for bringing us the good news telling us how to go about and carry on in this world.

Right: It is these who have tried to help us understand where we are and to carry ourselves in this creation.

Left: And so, to these beings, the messengers of the Creator,

Leader: we put our minds together as one mind and extend a greeting and a thanksgiving.

Leader: And now there is the Creator, the great mystery.

Right: It is the Creator that brought us all of these things and we know that all that is necessary for life and happiness is provided for us.

Left: And it is true that no one will know the Creator's face as we travel about on this earth, but that the Creator simply asks us to greet one another and be thankful and grateful to all that we see about us, for they are the ones who give us life.

Leader: And so as we gather here, we put our minds together as one mind and extend a greeting and thanksgiving to our Creator.

And now, if there is anything that has been left out and the people listening have remembered a special thing that should receive a greeting and a thanksgiving, it should be remembered that we have not learned all to which we are to give greetings; other times we are forgetful. If there are things that have been left out, now is the time to extend a special greeting and thanksgiving.

APPENDIX C

Native American Quiz

1. The Pomo Basket is a story nearly lost to history but is one that is instructive in understanding traditional Native cultural practices. For Indian girls to learn how to weave a basket is to learn a marketable craft.

   T F

2. At the time of Columbus' arrival in America, there were approximately 100 million Native Americans. The 2000 figures show the Native populations in the United States at about:

   a. 10 million c. 4 million

   b. 6 million d. 2 million

3. During the treaty making period between 1776 and 1871, the United States entered into well over _______ treaties with Native American tribes and nations.

   a. 100 c. 300

   b. 200 d. 400

4. In the case of the Plains Indians, what finally caused defeat was:

   a. Killing of the buffalo b. The strength of the military

   c. The killing of their leaders d. Building fences along the rivers

5. In 1970s, Congress heard testimony of the work of American drug companies who used Indian school children to test new drugs before marketing.

   T F

6. There are 562 federally recognized tribes or nations in the United States.

   T F

7. Many of the problems Native Americans struggle with are a result of poverty. Alcoholism is ________% higher than national average and diabetes is _____% higher.

   a. 200 c. 600

   b. 350 d. 950

8. All Native American tribes have Powwows.

   T F

9. ___________ has the largest number of tribes. ____________ has the largest population of Native people.

   a. Alaska c. North Carolina

   b. South Dakota d. Oklahoma

10. One in four (25%) of American Indian women in the U.S. live in poverty.

    T F

11. Only 83% of Native American mothers begin prenatal care in the first trimester of pregnancy.

    T F

12. Native American women in Oklahoma are twice as likely to experience domestic violence as the average American woman.

    T F

Answers: Native American Quiz

1. **FALSE.** Because of the tradition of baskets being used for utilitarian purposes as well as to teach young Indian girls, learning to weave the baskets is to learn about the whole world.

2. **C – 4 million.** The Native American population has been killed, forced into slavery, or died from diseases after the arrival of Europeans.

3. **D – 400 treaties.** However, as more and more people came to America, they moved westward encroaching on Native American lands and depleting/destroying resources, and breaking treaties so as to have more land, mine gold and build an infrastructure to support the migration west.

4. **A – Killing the buffalo.** The Plains Indians were hunters and dependent on buffalo for food, clothing and so forth.

5. **TRUE.** This speaks to the value that has been placed on our Native American brothers and sisters.

6. **TRUE.** However, we have tribes not federally recognized for a variety of reasons. Some have never had a treaty with the federal government or lived on a reservation; some have lost their traditions, cultures and language causing questions to arise as to whether they truly are Native American.

7. **D – 950%** **B – 350%**

8. **FALSE.** While some tribes continue to have powwows as a part of their tradition, many do not. Powwows are one way of meeting new people.

9. **A – Alaska 230 tribes** **D – Oklahoma**

10. **TRUE.** The number is even greater for Native American single mothers: more than one third (38 percent) of families headed by a Native American single mother live in poverty. (—Institute for Women's Policy Research)

11. **FALSE.** Only 69 percent of Native American mothers begin prenatal care in the first trimester of pregnancy, compared with 83 percent of all women.

12. **TRUE.** Native American women are twice as likely to experience domestic violence as the average American woman. 39 percent are victims of domestic violence. (The National Coalition Against Domestic Violence website.)

APPENDIX D

On the Air with NAUM: "Native Americans and the United Methodist Church Today"

Cast

Moderator

Host Sarah

Betty Hodson, Navajo and Kansas West UMW president

Wilma Mankiller, former Cherokee chief

Gary Locklear, Lumbee missionary

Fran Lynch

Choose one other from Appendix E.

Two announcers for commercial breaks.

Studio audience: remaining participants (some will have signed up to share in one to two minutes what that learned about Native Americans in their conference/area).

Set

In the front of the "stage," set up five to seven chairs for the moderator and four to six interviewees. To one side, set up two chairs for the announcers of commercials.

Host Sarah: Welcome to NAUM where we are broadcasting live tonight. I am your host, Sarah, and we will be talking with our special guests on "Native Americans and the United Methodist Church Today." We will also hear some personal experiences of our studio audience.

Let us begin today with our first guest. She currently serves as the Kansas West Conference President, Betty Hodson. She is a member of the Navajo Indian tribe and has quite a story to tell. *(turning to Betty)* Betty, thank you so much for taking time out of your busy schedule to be with us and tell us of your journey.

Betty Hodsen: *(tells her story in the first person using the information in Appendix E)*

Host Sarah: We appreciate your sharing your story and helping us to understand some of the struggles, pain and joy in your lifetime.

It is now my pleasure to introduce to you another chief, Wilma Mankiller. She was the first Cherokee woman to be chief of the Cherokee Nation from 1985 -1995 *(turning to Wilma)*. Wilma Mankiller, you tell a story about your experience with a United Methodist mission and your journey to becoming chief. Would you share this with our audience?

Wilma Mankiller: *(tells her story in the first person using the information in Appendix E)*

Host Sarah: Thank you so much for sharing your journey with us and telling us how Cookson Hills Center in Oklahoma was there for you when you had nowhere else to turn.

(turning to the audience) Gary Locklear is our next guest. Gary is a Lumbee and serves as a Church and Community Worker, which is a missionary and Home Missioner of the General Board of Global Ministries. His assignment is to the Rockingham District Native American Cooperative Parish in North Carolina *(turning now to Gary Locklear)*. Gary, there are some pretty exciting things happening with the churches and the people in the parish who are Lumbees. Tell us how this got started and what is happening today.

Gary Locklear: *(tells in first person using the information found in the story in* New World Outlook*, July/August 2007.)*

Host Sarah: Thank you so much, Gary, for sharing the work you are doing and that of the parish churches. It shows how working together can really make a difference. However, before we go on, it is time for a commercial break:

Announcer # 1: Good afternoon, friends! We have a special for you at the corner Native Food Grocery in the deli. We just received a new shipment of Buffalo Jerky, a favorite and staple of our Indian tribes.

Announcer #2: Stop by today on your way home. The supply is limited!

Host Sarah: Before we hear from our remaining guests, let's go to the audience and hear from some of you. I understand *(name)* can tell us something about Native

Americans in her conference or area *(invite one participant to report, followed by a second. Limit reports to one to two minutes.)*

Host Sarah: Thank you so much for bringing us up to date on what is happening in your communities and conferences. Now, let us go back to our panelists and hear from Fran Lynch, a Deaconess and Church and Community Worker serving in Alaska. Fran, tell us how one of our missionaries ended up serving in Willow and two communities in the bush.

Fran Lynch: *(tells her story in the first person using the information in the story in Appendix E, "Mission in the Alaska Bush")*

Host Sarah: *(to audience)* Well, it's exciting to see our church responding to the request of the parents, don't you agree? We're glad to know the church has been there for the long haul with a consistent presence. Thank you so much, Fran.

(turning to the audience) It's time for another commercial break. But don't go away, we'll be right back!

Announcer #1: Are you looking for a special, munchy treat for the trip home? Come on by the corner Native Food Grocery and pick up a bag of Maple Popcorn Balls!

Announcer #2: *(pretends to be sampling popcorn ball)* This is a mouth-watering treat from our agrarian Native peoples. Uuum, uuummm, Good! Don't miss this chance to get some of these popcorn balls made with real maple syrup.

Host Sarah: We have one more special guest, ____________ We are so glad you have been able to join us and share your faith journey. *(turning to ____________: (tells her story in the first person using the information in the story in Appendix E)*

Host Sarah: Thank you so much for sharing your story. We wish you well as you continue your journey in service and ministry. Well, we just have time to hear from a few more of our studio audience before we go. *(call by name two to four more participants)*

I am afraid our time is up. But before we go, let's have a show of hands of everyone who learned you have Native American ministries happening in your area. If you would just stand and tell us the name of the ministry and where it is located? *(give a couple minutes for participants who have not had a chance to share to stand now and give just the name and location of a ministry and Natives within the area)*

Once again, a big thank you to our special guests. *(Applause)* And thank you to all our studio audience and a special thanks to those of you who shared your stories. *(Applause)*

This is your Host Sarah saying thank you from all of us at NAUM for being with us today. Goodbye for now!

APPENDIX E

Vignettes

CHIEF SEATTLE (SEALTH)

How can you buy or sell the sky–the warmth of the land? The idea is strange to us. We do not own the freshness of the air or the sparkle of the water. How can you buy them from us?... We know that the white man does not understand our way. One portion of the land is the same to him as the next, for he is a stranger who comes in the night and takes from the land whatever he needs. The earth is not his brother but his enemy, and when he has conquered it, he moves on. He leaves his father's graves, and his children's birthright is forgotten...

There is no quiet place in the white man's cities. No place to hear the leaves of spring or the rustle of insect's wings. But perhaps because I am a savage and do not understand, the clatter only seems to insult the ears. And what is there to life if a man cannot hear the lovely cry of whippoorwill or the arguments of the frogs around a pond at night? The Indian prefers the soft sound of the wind darting over the face of the pond, and the smell of the wind itself cleansed by a midday rain, or scented with the piñon pine. The air is precious to the red man. For all things share the same breath–the beasts, the trees, the man. The white man does not seem to notice the air he breathes. Like a man dying for many days, he is numb to the stench. . .

When the last red man has vanished from the earth, and the memory is only the shadow of a cloud moving across the prairie, these shores and forests will still hold the spirits of my people, for they love this earth as the newborn loves its mother's heartbeat...One thing we know–out God is the same. This earth is precious to Him. Even the white man cannot be exempt from the common destiny.

–Sealth, a Duwamish chief, 1865

WILLIE AND HELEN SENUNGETUK

I met Willie and Helen Senungetuk in Nome, Alaska, in January of 1977. Born in the village of Wales in the early 1900s, this Inupiat couple had been childhood sweethearts. They had seen enough of life to discourage any of us. Before their children were born, they witnessed the terrible influenza epidemic in 1918 that killed more than one-third of the village's population of 600. Most of them died within a week. Having married and with children in tow, they moved to Nome so their children could receive an education. Willie and Helen concluded that the subsistence days of Arctic survival were coming to a close and their children needed new survival tools in the world. Willie became the janitor of the Nome high school but both Willie and Helen continued some of their subsistence practices that included a fish camp on the edge of the Bering Sea. There every harvest season one could see racks and rows of pink salmon drying in the longer days of late summer.

Our first meeting in 1977 was in their home. Crunching over the ice in the afternoon darkness of Arctic night, chilled by -40 degree temperatures, I was warmly greeted by Willie and Helen and offered magnificent hospitality. After comforting ourselves in each other's company, they told me about their life journey and how committed they were to the United Methodist/Presbyterian church of Nome they had attended from the time of their arrival as young parents. Willie was a revered elder in the Inupiat community, and I was surprised that he seemed humbled to have me in his home representing the larger church. "No one has done this before," he said. The formality didn't last long as we traded stories about Native life and the importance of the church and how we were working to mount strong Native advocacy programs. Willie was still the janitor of the school and was proud that he had never missed a day of work. He and Helen had raised their children in a traditional way and they had gone to university to obtain the survival tools for the new age. Now Willie was focusing his leadership role in the community on the prospects of oil companies moving in and despoiling the sea and the tundra. His children were doing their best to speak a new language about survival. Two of them were major artists and university teachers making their statements about Native issues and symbols of the new world crashing upon Native communities bringing disease, addiction and suicide

Our friendship continued for over ten years until Willie entered the Native Hospital in Anchorage. He would not leave alive. I remember stuffing seal oil and walrus fat into the overhead storage in my flight from Nome to Anchorage one day. The family wanted Willie to have some of his Native food while he was hospitalized because he was homesick. It was a warm summer day and by the time we arrived in Anchorage, the tourists on the plane were trying to figure out where the unusual scent was coming from. Willie loved the food. Later, in a visit to the hospital, I learned that Willie had been asked to address the youth in the Elders' Conference in Nome. He was determined to get there. He had been practicing his speech in bed and was preparing to leave the hospital when he had a setback that would not allow him to travel home. One afternoon, I took a little tape recorder to Willie and suggested he might like to tape his speech in the event he was not able to travel to the conference. He picked it up and with disgust shoved it to the bottom of his bed. He would get there. We talked through the afternoon until his supper arrived and I said I would leave and give him some rest. As I rose, Willie picked up the tape recorder and said, "How do you run this thing?" I showed him and said I would wait outside so he could record his speech. As I walked down the hall, I could hear Willie challenging the youth not to take helicopter rides with oil companies and to keep their Native life undisturbed and care for the animals and the land. Some weeks later, Willie's speech was played for the youth in the Elders' Conference. Willie had passed on.

JENNIFER BATTIEST

My grandmother was very influential in my life. She was very active in church and encouraged me in my faith. She was also active in the UMW on local, and conference levels to which she always took me or my brother to the meetings with her. The United Methodist Women of my home conference have also been very influential and supportive. They and my grandmother told me that I was talented, creative and that I could grow to be whatever I wanted to be. And I believed them.

Since I was a young child I have always wanted to be a missionary. I have no clear memory of where I heard the word nor did I have a clear understanding of the meaning. I thought a missionary was a person who worked with the church and that's what I wanted to do.

In college, I continued exploring what I wanted to do with my life. I heard about the Summer Mission Intern program through the General Board of Global Ministries. I applied and served as a summer intern. While in this position, I learned about the US2 program with Global Ministries in my search as to what I wanted to do next with my life. As a Choctaw young woman, I became the first Native American to serve as a US2 and was assigned to serve with the Robeson County Church and Community Center in North Carolina. To this day, receiving the anchor cross during my commissioning as a symbol of my being in mission service is one of my most cherished memories.

Once again, as I continued my journey, I applied and was hired to be one of two Missionaries In Residence with the General Board of Global Ministries Young Adult program. I felt I would be beneficial in helping to restructure the program.

As my term as an MIR came to an end, I decided I wanted to go to seminary and ended up at Drew where I continued my discernment. Upon graduation in October 2006, I went back to the

Oklahoma Indian Missionary Conference. I was approached by the Conference Superintendent, David Wilson, and the NW District Superintendent (Margaret Battiest, who happens to be my mother) and asked to take this little tiny church. (laughs) It only had two children coming but they kept coming when no one else came—every Sunday. I said, "How can I say no to this? Someone needs to be there consistently," so I said yes and I was appointed part time as pastor. It is growing slowly – the two children started bringing their 2 year old sister and were joined by 6 other children and an adult. At annual conference, I was appointed as a full time pastor to a two point charge, one of which is the church of the children. I still think of myself as a missionary rather than as clergy. I am still discerning as to where I want to go. I do not know yet where my journey is leading but it will be in service through the church – as a missionary or ordained elder is yet to be decided.

BETTY HODSGEN

I am a member of the Navajo Indian tribe and my clan is the Redhouse Clan. I currently serve as Conference President of United Methodist Women in the Kansas West Conference. In 1929, I was born in Shiprock, New Mexico on the Navajo reservation of a Navajo father and a white mother. I never was very fluent in the language of my tribe, which is a very difficult one. The only identity card that has any reference to my being Indian is my Social Security card with my Indian census number on it. I had two sisters and a brother who all had Indian census numbers, as does my son. My parents lived their whole lives on the reservation.

In 1935 when I was six, my parents enrolled my cousin and me at the Navajo Methodist Mission School, Farmington, New Mexico so that we could have a better education than was available in the government school in my hometown. We were allowed to go home overnight twice a year. Yes, I cried many tears but surprisingly, I soon adjusted and never questioned what my parents chose to do. My sisters and brother all attended the school as well. My parents visited us weekly during the school year.

The school made a difference in our lives—many of our graduates went on to college, some got Master's degrees, and several became leaders in our tribe. The first Navajo doctor graduated from the school and one of the girls I attended school with did tremendous work in education on the reservation. A school in my home town is named after her. Not everyone chose this path. One of my best friends left the school and chose to raise a family on the reservation while affirming Navajo dress and traditions.

At my arrival for school, I had my first taste of racial discrimination, not from white people but from my full- blooded Navajo peers who found out I was part white. They soon taunted me by calling me "little white person." To them that was the worst thing they could call me. My brother remembers being called "half breed" in his younger years at school. I felt differences because of my mixed race, and also because I was a girl. There definitely were more privileges given the boys than the girls. On campus, girls had a line of demarcation we were not to go past, but the boys could go anywhere they wanted.

Some Indians have attended boarding schools administered by the government or other church denominations and have not had pleasant experiences. My memories of the Mission, as we call it, were of those staff members who loved us as though we were their own children; who taught us so diligently and thoroughly that we were prepared to attend college if we chose to do so; who saw to our spirituality development through Bible study as a part of the school curriculum and guided us through commitment to the Lord Jesus Christ; who saw that we understood the value of discipline; who taught work ethics through various duties performed about the campus; who instilled the responsibility of doing homework; and who, along with my parents, made me the person I am today. I went to McPherson College in Kansas and graduated in 1951. Employment at the Boeing Company began in 1952 where I worked my way through glass ceilings and retired in a 1992 as a third level manager in Industrial Engineering.

Yes, I have experienced racial injustice from time to time. When there was downsizing at my job, I was not impacted. But word got around that this had nothing to do with my performance, it was only because I was Indian. I have been passed up for next-in-line service at restaurants (though not so much anymore, thankfully), and have experienced being "overlooked" when it was my turn to pay for my purchases in a department store. Despite or because of this, I am personally committed to working towards racial justice for all.

I love being a United Methodist Woman and I love the United Methodist Church. I do believe I understand what being in mission is and I will be forever grateful for what mission monies have done for me. The opportunity for me to serve as an officer at the Conference UMW was a long time coming. I spent several years serving on committees, until one day during a Charter for Racial Justice Committee meeting, I asked what I had to do as a person of color to qualify to be an officer, besides committee service. I also expressed that I did not believe measures were being take to develop women of color to be leaders. About a year or so after that, my opportunity came when I was asked to serve as Membership Nurture and Outreach Mission Coordinator and then four years later, as President. I am the first woman of color to serve as president of our conference. When the gavel was passed to me, I stated that I always wanted to be an Indian Chief and now I am one.

It has not been difficult to maintain my Navajo identity when I do not live on the reservation. I serve on the Kansas West Conference Native American Ministries Committee and let it be known that I am a member of the Navajo Indian tribe. Recently, the chairperson of this committee and I helped two churches celebrate Native American Ministries Sunday. We both dressed in the garb of our respective tribes. We had a great time doing this. I am also a charter member of the Wichita Mid-America All Indian Center.

At last there is a School of Christian Mission study to enlighten one and all about the plight of Native Americans in the past and more importantly, what oversight our peoples continue to endure in the current day and age.

NELLIE LONG

My name is Nellie Long and I serve as the Conference Mission Coordinator for Social Action in the Oklahoma Indian Missionary Conference. Within the conference we have more than 39 tribes, and many different languages among us. Each tribe has different traditions and cultures. I am from the Choctaw tribe of Oklahoma. I live in Oklahoma City with my husband who is Creek-speaking, but is a member of the Sac and Fox Nation.

It's hard for some people to realize that we are the original inhabitants here. Today we live a reality different than anyone else in the US. We often feel invisible and are treated like second-class citizens. We carry [CDIB] government issued identity cards as well as Tribal cards that say what tribe we come from. These cards give us access to tribal healthcare and benefits. No other group in the US has to carry such an identity card to gain benefits. Many people simply don't know this fact.

For health care coverage we can go to the clinic of any tribe, but in order to get specialized care we need to apply to the Indian Health Service. It can take anywhere from two weeks to six months to get an approval.

Last summer my young niece broke her arm on a Friday evening. We took her to the emergency room of the city hospital. They said that she needed to see a pediatric orthopedic doctor. The Oklahoma City Indian clinic would not be open until the following Monday. When we called they said it could be two weeks until she could get a referral to see a specialist. She was referred to the Chickasaw Nation Indian hospital. We took her there and X-rays confirmed the break. But they couldn't help her because she was "out of area" in terms of people served by that institution. So she was referred to her own tribal Indian hospital in Okemah, OK.

Early the next morning we drove her the 80 miles to her tribal Indian hospital in Okemah. When we began to register her in the emergency room we gave her Oklahoma City address. They told us, "We can't help you because even though she's in the tribe, she lives out of the area." We then took her to my husband's tribal clinic who told her the same thing. We were getting the run around and she was not getting the care she needed. We kept being told she's in the wrong tribe or the wrong place. One way or the other, they denied her care. There was a time when it would not have mattered what tribe she was in. It seems that with funding cuts the hospitals are limiting their delivery to a specific geographic area.

Finally, we brought her back to the Children's Hospital in town. When they saw the arm and how long she had gone without receiving attention, the health professionals yelled at us and blamed us for not getting her to a doctor. They assumed that we had neglected the child and were not caring for her, when we had spent the past three days going from hospital to hospital trying to get care that was needed. They even threatened to call the child welfare authorities on us for lack of attention. These are the kinds of assumptions made about Indians that we often experience. She finally got attention, but we had to pay for it out of pocket. We were not able to get the emergency care from our tribal facilities.

The Children's Defense Fund is advocating for health coverage for all children. If we succeeded in this goal it would ensure that Indian kids and all kids would not face this kind of dilemma. Our Indian health care is of no value if we can't see the doctors we need to see, including specialists. Many Indians purchase private health insurance or get it through their work, because Indian healthcare is so limited. But some of us can't afford private insurance. Me and my children and grandkids don't have insurance. My husband has Medicare.

We are indigenous peoples who have been displaced, marginalized and impoverished. The state and tribes issue Native identity cards that may limit the quality of health care and other benefits that we can receive. We have deep pride in our heritage and ancestors. But it is a different thing to have the state bestow an "identity" on us, where we carry the stigma of an identity card for services. It is a very painful reminder of our second-class citizenship in this country.

MISSION IN THE ALASKA BUSH

The Church and Community Ministry in the Athabaskan Indian bush villages of Anvik and Grayling, Alaska is a ministry of presence. I have been going for over ten years to have Sunday School with the children. At first they were always surprised each month and would say "You came back!" Now if I miss a month they say, "Where have you been?" In these small, isolated villages, many people have come and gone. School teachers and workers for special projects are generally short term folks. The children have to get used to meeting new people on a regular basis. They sometimes think something is wrong with them or that they have done something wrong to make the people leave. It is difficult to get attached if they know a person is just passing through. When I first started going, the Tribal Administrator in Anvik told me to hang in there and keep coming back, even when Sunday School did not go smoothly. That's what I have done.

Relationships have developed between the children, their parents, grandparents, and me. We know each other and can trust each other. I make my rounds of visits when I am in the villages. We talk about life and how the current batch of Sunday School children are doing. How are those children who have grown up, and what choices are they making as adults? I now have the children of some of the first children I had in Sunday School. We talk about who is sick, what families are breaking up, and who is moving to town or going in to wait for their baby to be born. Is the fishing good? Are the bears out? Did everyone get their moose?

This past week I shared an experience for the first time with the folks in Grayling. We had just finished Sunday School and the children were leaving. They came running back into the Bingo Hall yelling, "Fran, the ice is running!" I ran out with them to join the large group of people on the banks of the Yukon River to watch this humongous sheet of ice moving at a fast clip down the river. This was not the scene of a large body of open water with some large ice chunks floating by. This was a river of ice moving, pushing whatever was in its path. It was one of the most powerful images I have experienced in a while. There were cracks as ice piled up on ice and loud swishing sounds as ice pushed and passed other ice. Over the course of the hour that we stood and watched, a mountain of ice grew at a bend in the river and eventually stopped the ice from running. We gasped, shouted, laughed, and pointed. Even those who see it run every year were excited. With the ice moving we could say spring is here. The salmon will be running next. Life is good. The next day in Sunday School we talked about the power of the river and the joy of summer. We talked about the power of God and the joy of being loved and of loving others. It's a ministry of presence. You are there for the long haul. We share experiences. We build a relationship. We share and experience God's love.

—Fran Lynch, Church and Community Worker, a missionary and Deaconess of the General Board of Global Ministries

WILMA MANKILLER

I want to share out of a story with you from an experience I had this morning. I received an email from someone saying a teacher in the state of Pennsylvania had taken a survey of the children asking them to name a contemporary Native American. Over half of them named me and I was the only one many of them could think of. I want to share with you how I went to that point from being a divorced mother of two looking for a job in eastern Oklahoma and what it has to do with the United Methodist Church.

In 1976, my two daughters and I returned to Oklahoma after having lived in California for almost twenty years. I had no job, I had no idea of what I would do, no car and no money – I just knew it was time to come home. We were staying with my mother while I was looking for a job and trying to get my children in school. An elder Cherokee woman told my mother and me she knew of a place where I could go to get some work clothes for myself, school clothes for the children and some help. So I went to Cookson Hills Center. I expected to pay a small amount for the clothes and was surprised when they gave me the clothes for myself and my children and some other things we needed to get started in Oklahoma. They were so loving and kind – they didn't ask if I was a United Methodist and they didn't ask much else – they just knew I was a single mother with two daughters and they needed to go to school and I needed a job and they could help.

And I was successful in getting a job. I took a job with the Cherokee Nation and later ended up leading the Cherokee Nation. I think that is an important story to tell. I think everyone should realize we live in a reciprocal society and reciprocal world and sometimes people need help and they lean on others and sometimes those others lean on them when they need help and that's how we get by in society. And there was a point in time when I needed to lean on others and I leaned on the Cookson Hills Mission Center for help and they did help. It was a good lesson for me to learn and I still try to help people every day of my life through the years as the Cookson Hills Center is one of the groups of people that helped me.

— As told by Wilma Mankiller, first woman Cherokee Chief, 1985-1995

SAND CREEK MASSACRE

It was an honor to represent the United Methodist Commission on Christian Unity and Interreligious Concerns at the April 28 memorial dedication of the Sand Creek Massacre National Historic Site near Chivington, Colorado

Chivington is a small, dusty town that has no retail businesses whatsoever and only a few sand-beaten dwellings. This town is named for Colonel John Chivington, who led the 1864 massacre of Cheyenne and Arapaho innocents.

It is because of Chivington that I, a United Methodist, found myself in this remote territory. A strange tie binds me to Chivington and to the two hundred who died at Sand Creek.

My tie to Chivington is that we are both Methodists and both preachers. I am left with questions: By what set of circumstances did this Methodist Episcopal pastor give up his Christian ministry and choose a path of violence—not a battle, but a vigilante massacre? And what happens to a man's spirit that he looks upon the perfect little faces of Indian children and says, "Nits make lice," ordering his men to kill them all?

I am not sure, but I am reminded that sin abides in us all, and evil can and will assert itself even through the very vessels which hold the souls of Christians.

My personal connection to the Massacre of 1864 is that I am Native American as well as a Methodist. My knowledge of the massacre dates back to my teen years, when our pastor showed the movie "Soldier Blue" to our youth fellowship group. The graphic images of that film have stayed with me over thirty-five years.

Another connection is that I had a friend, Dee Wright, a Pawnee Indian who was one of the last living members of the Pawnee Bill Wild West. I remember him telling me about a good friend of his who had escaped the Sand Creek Massacre at the age of seven. Dee said this friend had hidden in the creek, breathing through a reed for a day and night before daring to move. You don't forget images like these.

Descendants of the massacre survivors—Northern and Southern Arapahos, Northern and Southern Cheyenne—made the pilgrimage to Colorado, camping and praying along the now-dry creek bed.

With steady drumbeat, the singers sang old songs, including the actual death song of White Antelope, which he sang while lying at the edge of Sand Creek. It is still remembered in this most sacred oral tradition.

About two thousand persons attended the ceremonials, which lasted from early morning till dark. In the evening, we were honored by descendants who danced gourd dances and round dances.

Darrell Flyingman, governor of the Southern Arapaho and Southern Cheyenne tribes, described the days of encampment and ceremonies by noting that "we were welcomed by our ancestors and our relatives." U.S. Sen. Sam Brownback, (R-Kan.), brought the words "I apologize deeply. Forgive us."

It has become clear that words are not enough. At the 1996 United Methodist General Conference in Denver, a resolution was adopted to support government restitutions to the Cheyenne and Arapaho Tribes for wrongs against humanity, but the statement offered only words from our church. A new resolution is being brought to the 2008 General Conference seeking financial support for this national historic site.

As a nation, we have come to this good day when we do acknowledge and remember what happened at Sand Creek. A monument will be built at the site, and perhaps of equal importance, a research center is being established in the nearby town of Eads, dedicated to not only this particular event, but also to the study of genocide. The park service is providing matching funds for donations to the project.

We envision Indians and non-Indians coming to the site will remember what happened at Sand Creek. We envision scholars and students, pastors and church folk coming to learn the truth of history and to continue raising the important questions lest we repeat the sins of our forebears. It is time for more than words.

Carole Lakota Eastin is the pastor of the Native American Fellowship—Dayspring United Methodist Church near Peoria, Ill., and a director of the United Methodist Commission on Christian Unity and Interreligious Concerns.

— News media contact: Linda Bloom, New York, (646) 369-3759 or HYPERLINK "mailto:newsdesk@umcom.org" newsdesk@umcom.org.

APPENDIX F

United Methodist Resolutions on Native Americans

130. CONCERNING DEMEANING NAMES TO NATIVE AMERICANS

In our society today, there is a growing debate and discussion about the appropriateness of using Native American names as nicknames for professional sports teams and university mascots. As the publication *Words That Hurt, Words That Heal*, produced by The United Methodist Church, highlights, the use of names and language is a powerful instrument for good and destructive purposes. It is demeaning to Native Americans and other members of our society to depict Native Americans as violent and aggressive people by calling a sports team the "Braves" or the "Warriors." The implication is that all Native Americans are aggressive and violent people. This use of nicknames is not conducive to the development of a society committed to the common good of its citizenry.

In "The United Methodist Church and America's Native People" (The Book of Resolutions, 1992; page 178), The United Methodist Church has issued a call for repentance for the church's role in the dehumanization and colonization of our Native American sisters and brothers. In light of this stand and the fact that we strongly believe the continued use of Native American names as nicknames is demeaning and racist, we urge all United Methodist-related universities, colleges, and schools to set an example by replacing any nicknames that demean and offend our Native American sisters and brothers; and we support efforts throughout our society to replace such nicknames, mascots, and symbols.

ADOPTED 1996, READOPTED 2004

See Social Principles, ¶ 162A.

134. HEALTH CARE FOR NATIVE AMERICANS

WHEREAS, Native Americans are the most socio-economically deprived minority group in the United States; and

WHEREAS, the United States government is bound by treaty to provide health care for all Native Americans; and

WHEREAS, the United States government now provides these medical services through Indian

Health Services, United States Public Health Service, Department of Health and Human Services; and

WHEREAS, medical services currently provided by the Indian Health Services for health education and prenatal care have contributed to a rapid decline in infant mortality among Native Americans; and

WHEREAS, similar successes of these health programs are likely to have occurred for all Native Americans living in the United States; and

WHEREAS, despite these successes, the federal government is constantly threatening to cut the Indian Health Services Program; and

WHEREAS, any funding cuts could severely curtail or cancel health care for a large number of eligible Native Americans; and

WHEREAS, a small number of Native Americans can afford to buy private health insurance,

Therefore, be it resolved, that all Native Americans have access to adequate medical services to ensure a balance of physical, mental, and spiritual well-being for the "Journey Toward Wholeness;" and that the United States Congress allows no decrease in federal funds to operate Indian health facilities.

Be it further resolved, that the General Board of Church and Society submit this resolution, on behalf of the General Conference, to all United States senators and legislators who have Indian Health Services within their respective state.

ADOPTED 1988, AMENDED AND READOPTED 2000

See Social Principles, ¶ 162A.

137. NATIVE AMERICAN MINISTRIES SUNDAY

WHEREAS, the Native American population continues to shift in larger numbers from the rural areas to the urban population centers; and

WHEREAS, the human conditions of numerous Native Americans in the rural and urban environments reflect a legacy of poverty and socioeconomic denial; and

WHEREAS, there is a serious shortage of Native American pastors and trained professionals to respond to the human conditions in the Native American communities; and

WHEREAS, there is a National United Methodist Native American Center, which has been created to recruit, train, and deploy Native American leadership; and

WHEREAS, the financial support that is required to sustain the center is beyond the capability of the Native American communities; and

WHEREAS, the 1988 General Conference approved Native American Awareness Sunday (now known as N.A.M. Sunday) as a means for providing opportunities for the denomination to support Native American ministries;

Therefore, be it resolved, that all annual conferences promote the observance of the Native American Ministries Sunday and encourage local churches to support the Sunday with programming and offerings.

Be it further resolved, that the agencies that develop and provide resources for this special day report to the General Commission on Religion and Race their plans, strategies, and timelines for addressing the goals and objectives related to Native American Ministries Sunday.

ADOPTED 1992, READOPTED 2004

See Social Principles, ¶ 162A

143. NATIVE AMERICAN RELIGIOUS FREEDOM ACT

WHEREAS, tribal people have gone into the high places, lakes, and isolated sanctuaries to pray, receive guidance from God, and train younger people in the ceremonies that constitute the spiritual life of Native American communities; and

WHEREAS, when tribes were forcibly removed from their homelands and forced to live on restricted reservations, many of the ceremonies were prohibited; and

WHEREAS, most Indians do not see any conflict between their old beliefs and the new religion of the Christian church; and

WHEREAS, during this century the expanding national population and the introduction of corporate farming and more extensive mining and timber industry activities reduced the isolation of rural America, making it difficult for small parties of Native Americans to go into the mountains or to remote lakes and buttes to conduct ceremonies without interference from non-Indians; and

WHEREAS, federal agencies began to restrict Indian access to sacred sites by establishing increasingly narrow rules and regulations for managing public lands; and

WHEREAS, in 1978, in an effort to clarify the status of traditional Native American religious practices and practitioners, Congress passed a Joint Resolution entitled "The American Indian Religious Freedom Act," which declared that it was the policy of Congress to protect and preserve the inherent right of Native Americans to believe, express, and practice their traditional religions; and

WHEREAS, today a major crisis exists in that there is no real protection for the practice of traditional Indian religions within the framework of American constitutional or statutory law, and courts usually automatically dismiss Indian petitions without evidentiary hearings; and

WHEREAS, while Congress has passed many laws that are designed to protect certain kinds of lands and resources for environmental and historic preservation, none of these laws is designed to protect the practice of Indian religion on sacred sites; and

WHEREAS, the only existing law directly addressing this issue, the American Indian Religious Freedom Act, is simply a policy that provides limited legal relief to aggrieved American Indian religious practitioners,

Therefore, be it resolved, that the General Board of Global Ministries and the General Board of Church and Society make available to the church information on the American Indian Religious Freedom Act; and

Be it further resolved, that the General Board of Church and Society support legislation that will provide for a legal cause of action when sacred sites may be affected by governmental action; proposed legislation should also provide for more extensive notice to and consultation with tribes and affected parties; and

Be it further resolved, that the General Board of Church and Society may enter and support court cases relating to the American Indian Religious Freedom Act; and

Be it further resolved, that the General Board of Church and Society communicate with the Senate Committee on Indian Affairs, declaring that the position of The United Methodist Church, expressed through the 1992 General Conference, is to strengthen the American Indian Religious Freedom Act of 1978 and preserve the God-given and constitutional rights of religious freedom for Native Americans.

ADOPTED 1992, AMENDED AND READOPTED 2004

See Social Principles, ¶ 162A

Order the following from the Mission Resource Center (1-800- 305-9857 or www.missionresourcecenter.org).

Creator Sang a Welcoming Song: Native America for Children by Ray Buckley.
This four-session study for children is intended as a gift from Native people. While children will learn something of the Native histories and cultures, it is intended to be far more than a classroom experience. Through relational, interactive experiences, children will discover the "Welcoming Song" that the Creator sings for them and for all of God's children. (**#M3021**) $8.00

Walking in These White Man Shoes: Youth Explore Native America by Ray Buckley.
"Walking in these white man shoes" refers to the Native experience of trying to live in two worlds, one of which didn't quite fit. In this study, youth are invited to walk with Native people as they hear the story of where Native people have walked, where they are walking now, and how they walk with God. Includes a four-session study guide. (**#M3022**) $8.00

Stories from the Circle of Life DVD
Tells stories of Native Americans throughout the United States. Native narratives explore faith journeys; ways they have integrated cultural beliefs into faith and life; issues confronting communities historically and today; and lessons for the church and all God's people. Includes a guide for discussion and reflection and an audio version of the study book Giving Our Hearts Away by Thom White Wolf Fassett. DVD approximately 37 minutes; audio book 4 hours. (**#M3016**) $19.95

North American Indian Reference Map
This informative and illustrative map displays the history and evolution of Native American land and the linguistic families of Native Americans at the time of the first European contact. Through supplemental text, illustrations and photos, the history, leaders, innovations and culture of the North American Indians is thoroughly told. National Geographic, 2004, 31" x 20". (**#M3024**) $12.00

NOTES